# Qlik Sense® Coo

Over 80 step-by-step recipes to tackle the everyday
challenges faced by Qlik Sense® developers

**Philip Hand**

**Neeraj Kharpate**

BIRMINGHAM - MUMBAI

# Qlik Sense® Cookbook

First published: November 2015

Production reference: 1251115

Published by Packt Publishing Ltd.
Livery Place
35 Livery Street
Birmingham B3 2PB, UK.

ISBN 978-1-78217-514-8

www.packtpub.com

# Credits

**Authors**

Philip Hand

Neeraj Kharpate

**Reviewers**

Steve Dark

Holly A. Kraig-Helton

Pablo Labbe Ibaceta

Stefan Stoichev

**Commissioning Editor**

Neil Alexander

**Acquisition Editor**

Kevin Colaco

**Content Development Editor**

Adrian Raposo

**Technical Editor**

Saurabh Malhotra

**Copy Editor**

Sneha Singh

**Project Coordinator**

Sanchita Mandal

**Proofreaders**

Safis Editing

**Indexers**

Hemangini Bari

Tejal Daruwale Soni

**Graphics**

Kirk D'Penha

**Production Coordinator**

Shantanu N. Zagade

**Cover Work**

Shantanu N. Zagade

# Foreword

It has been an interesting few years for someone who has been very close to what Qlik has been doing with its products and in the market place. Their core product has evolved slowly and gained few new features at each release, while other products were gaining ground. Supporters of these other products talk of better visualizations and a more seamless integration with the web—which is after all where we live our lives these days. As Qlik followers, we were given talk of a roadmap of what was then known as Next and some glimpses of the UI that is built for mobile first and is fully responsive might look like. The gap between QlikView and these concepts seemed quite wide at the time. Was Qlik going to be able to bridge the gap and take their offering forward?

It was July 2014 when the desktop only version of Qlik Sense made its first appearance. Here you could see the responsive UI, the ease with which things could be built, and you could certainly see that it was not a new version of QlikView. It whets the appetite for what was to come, but in many ways it raised more questions than it gave answers. So much of what the QlikView developers had come to take for granted had been taken away—the most curious omission from the initial release was the pivot table. Yet there were some similarities, which meant that porting things to this new product was relatively painless, the fact that the load script and expression syntax is almost identical certainly helped. The most important thing was, and still is, that at its core Qlik Sense has the same associative data model and the green, white, and grey selections are at the heart of QlikView.

While the initial release may have been met with skepticism by some (myself included), who have a history of creating applications in QlikView, there is no doubt that it heralded a sea of change in the amount of new features and innovation that came in with each Sense release.

The Sense Server became available with the initial desktop release, which allowed the creation of applications on any platform that has a browser and provides top class governance. The features that were obvious omissions from the initial release have made an appearance, for example pivot tables and variables. The product has expanded in various ways and more than what you might expect, such as the ability of an end user to pick their own colors for a chart even if they only have view access. Even after using the product for some time, it still has the ability to surprise me; for instance, the way the smart search knows the best way to interpret what I type in, even if they are vague. The snapshots and stories mean that more can be done without leaving the product, while the "single configurator" means that higher percentage of product can be embedded into other places.

The innovation and expansion didn't stop here either. Sense now powers the Qlik Cloud, a free to use service, where you can upload data and build and share visualizations right within your browser. This is where I get the most excited with where the things are headed; where previously the price tag of QlikView was a limiting factor outside of business, now anyone can explore data and display it in ways that make it meaningful. Simply put, they can master the building blocks of what makes a great BI app. The availability and ease of use of Qlik Cloud means that I have even been encouraging my children to use it for their homework. The barriers to the world of data discovery are being torn down. These are exciting times.

It is against this backdrop that the book you have in front you has been written. As each chapter was handed over for review, it seemed that another Sense version had been released and some buttons had moved from the location they were in, in the screenshot given in the draft. Various re-writes were required to refer to the latest Sense version, rather than the one that was out at the time of the first writing. The speed at which things are improving is fantastic to see—even if it's a bit frustrating for the authors of books on the subject! This constant innovation and improvement is evidenced in this book by the fact that a chapter was required at the end simply to cover the new features in the latest version—a sure sign of a vibrant product.

Whether you are shifting to Qlik Sense and are already familiar with QlikView or if you have come across it more recently, this book covers many things that you will need to know. From the simple use of the repositories and building straight forward dashboards to getting under the bonnet and building your own extensions, it is all here.

Sense is full of surprises and this book is your guide to unlocking some of the gems hidden within it. I hope you are ready to roll up your sleeves and get work with what is on offer.

Steve Dark

Director, Quick Intelligence Ltd

# About the Authors

**Philip Hand** is a senior business intelligence consultant who has worked with QlikView in the BI space for over 7 years. Working with Qlik's top partner in the UK, he has implemented end-to-end solutions in a wide variety of enterprises and for large business customers.

He is loathe to talk about himself in the third person but can be persuaded to do so from time to time. You can find him on Twitter at @QlikViewer.

He has a great experience and knowledge, as he has spent many years consulting in business and QlikView solutions. His belief is that such a role proves invaluable to hone your skills through exposure to many different businesses, problems, technologies, industries, and people.

He is an active member of the Qlik community and never misses a developer group (http://www.qlikdevgroup.com/). "Rugby lover", "Music lover", "Future dog owner".

I would like to thank my colleagues and customers, old and new, for all of the expert collaboration over the years. I'm proud to have made an impact on people and business in a positive way, as we all continue on our own journeys.

From my experience, stories of success are often stories of community. Business intelligence embodies this perfectly, from design, build, adoption, and success. Thank you to all of the small cogs!

Special thanks to three people— Stephen Redmond, a Qlik luminary from whom I have learned a lot working together over the years, Dilyana Ivanova, the first consultant I shadowed all these years, and one of the most intelligent and wonderful people I have had the pleasure of working with. Lastly, my coauthor and friend, Neeraj Kharpate.

**Neeraj Kharpate** works as a senior business intelligence consultant at Capventis (http://www.capventis.com), a QlikView Elite Partner. He started his career working as a technical support executive for an aviation ERP before embarking on his journey with QlikView in mid-2007. He has worked with many big ticket companies in India, Singapore, and the United Kingdom. He has over 8 years of experience in the field of QlikView implementations and training.

He is a certified Qlik Sense® Data architect, QlikView designer, developer, and trainer.

He has been following the developments in Qlik Sense® very closely, ever since it was launched in 2014 and is extremely excited about the future of this product.

He has done his masters in business administration at the Norwich Business School, University of East Anglia. He also has a diploma in management consulting from the Chartered Management Institute, UK. He has his first degree in Mechanical engineering from Nagpur University, India.

I would like to thank my family, especially my wife, Manik, who has been a constant source of encouragement during the writing of this book and my darling daughter, Ahaana, for being a good girl while daddy wrote the drafts.

I would also like to thank all my colleagues at Capventis who are a great team to work with.

A special thanks to Stephen Redmond, our former CTO whom I personally admire and who has been a great mentor during my journey with Capventis.

No theory can replace the knowledge I have gained working on site with all my wonderful customers. Heartfelt thanks!

Last but not the least, Mr. Philip Hand, the co-author of this book ..."Thanks mate. It was a great pleasure working with you on this book!"

# About the Reviewers

**Steve Dark** heads Quick Intelligence, a business intelligence consultancy with 100 percent focus on the Qlik platform. With clients in sectors as diverse as manufacturing, pharmaceuticals, and finance, they cover and support the entire Qlik project lifecycle and ecosystem for customers. Through the numerous successful implementations and challenges met for the clients; he has in depth expertise and a wealth of experience in QlikView and more recently, Qlik Sense®.

It is this experience that he shares through his blog at `http://www.quickintelligence. co.uk/qlikview-blog/` and via other channels, such as the Qlik Community. This sharing of knowledge and enthusiasm for the Qlik platform has been recognized by Qlik as they have made him a Luminary in 2014 and a Community MVP in 2015.

He has also been on the technical review team for *QlikView 11 for Developers*, *QlikView for Developers Cookbook*, *QlikView Scripting*, and *QlikView Server and Publisher*. All of these titles were published by Packt Publishing.

> I would like to thank all those colleagues and clients who have allowed me to keep doing the work that I enjoy, for so long.

**Holly A. Kraig-Helton** has over 16 years of experience in technical and digital content writing and over 5 years as an analyst. While her adventures in technology writing and editing started with writing tutorials on Windows 95 and using the Internet; her adventures eventually led her to work at Pearson Education and McGraw-Hill Publishing. Eventually, she took her wisdom gained in publishing and transferred it over to the entertainment and finance industries. Nowadays, you can find her pouring over data for a call-center and IVR system.

**Pablo Labbe Ibaceta** is a Business Intelligence consultant with over 15 years of experience. He has a strong knowledge of BI implementation methodology and project management working in the areas of retail, manufacturing, finance, and telecommunications.

In 2008 he was presented with QlikView, the former product by Qlik and the seed for Qlik Sense®. Since that year, he has been focused on delivering BI solutions in a new way.

He founded ANALITIKA Inteligencia (`http://www.analitika.com.br`) in 2014 to deliver BI projects focusing on Qlik products and other technologies that embrace the self-service BI. Their mission is to spread the information knowledge to all the levels of an organization. Since 2015 they have established a partnership with Qlik to be the official implementation partner.

He believes that Qlik Sense® enables true self-service BI + data visualization and discovery with unique capabilities and powered by the award-winning in-memory associative engine technology from his older brother QlikView.

He is an active member of the Brazilian Qlik Community and other social media sites. You can follow him on Twitter at `@pablolabbe` – where he tweets about Qlik, self service BI, data visualization, and other related technologies.

**Stefan Stoichev** has more than 8 years experience as a QlikView developer/consultant. He is currently working at Virgin Media UK as a senior QlikView analyst pushing Qlik View/Sense limits with big amounts of data.

I would like to thank Packt Publishing and the authors for the great book and of course to the people at Qlik for the great product.

# www.PacktPub.com

## Support files, eBooks, discount offers, and more

For support files and downloads related to your book, please visit www.PacktPub.com.

Did you know that Packt offers eBook versions of every book published, with PDF and ePub files available? You can upgrade to the eBook version at www.PacktPub.com and as a print book customer, you are entitled to a discount on the eBook copy. Get in touch with us at service@packtpub.com for more details.

At www.PacktPub.com, you can also read a collection of free technical articles, sign up for a range of free newsletters and receive exclusive discounts and offers on Packt books and eBooks.

https://www2.packtpub.com/books/subscription/packtlib

Do you need instant solutions to your IT questions? PacktLib is Packt's online digital book library. Here, you can search, access, and read Packt's entire library of books.

## Why subscribe?

- Fully searchable across every book published by Packt
- Copy and paste, print, and bookmark content
- On demand and accessible via a web browser

## Free access for Packt account holders

If you have an account with Packt at www.PacktPub.com, you can use this to access PacktLib today and view 9 entirely free books. Simply use your login credentials for immediate access.

## Instant updates on new Packt books

Get notified! Find out when new books are published by following @PacktEnterprise on Twitter or the *Packt Enterprise* Facebook page.

# Table of Contents

# Preface

Qlik is a market leader in the field of Business Discovery. As a company, it has been a pioneer when it comes to rapid returns on investment on business intelligence implementations. Its flagship product "QlikView" has been amongst the leaders in Gartner's magic quadrant for the past three consecutive years. This bears testimony to the fact that Qlik and its offerings have a wide-scale acceptability among business users.

The world of Business Intelligence has seen a paradigm shift over the last couple of years. With an increased level of market understanding and learning from customer experiences, Qlik has made significant developments in its product suite to suit the changing market demands.

With the evolving business scenario in mind, Qlik came up with "Qlik Sense®" in mid-2014. Qlik Sense® is a self-service data visualization platform; users can design their own applications using the simple drag and drop interface in Qlik Sense®. They can directly create their own applications on the web and share them through a centralized hub. A Qlik Sense® application can even be shared in the cloud.

A real thought process has been put into the development of Qlik Sense® according to what the businesses of today require. For example, there is a native "Map" object available in Qlik Sense® which stems from the need for Map extensions. The end users can edit the properties of the objects cn the screen directly through the interface. The "Qlik Dev Hub" provides a fast and easy approach to create extensions. In a way, Qlik Sense® gives the authority of the app to the end user and asks them to do their own data discovery in their own bespoke way.

Since the time of its launch, Qlik Sense® has garnered a huge interest in the business community and we have no doubt about its great future in the days to come. It has the capability to reach the depths of any organization very quickly and users will certainly love it.

This book uncovers all the wonderful features of this great product. It helps the user to overcome the challenges faced in day to day Qlik Sense® implementations. The solutions are discussed through simple and easy to understand recipes. We hope you find it useful.

# What this book covers

*Chapter 1*, *Getting Started with the Data*, introduces the user to different methods of loading data into Qlik Sense® from various sources, such as relational databases, data files and also custom databases, such as SAP. We will also delve into the creation and usage of a Master Library in Qlik Sense®.

*Chapter 2*, *Visualizations*, focuses on the best design practices in Qlik Sense® in order to create engaging applications. It also looks at the concept of snapshots and stories in Qlik Sense.

*Chapter 3*, *Scripting*, introduces the user to the techniques of writing a well-structured script in Qlik Sense®. It discusses and explains the benefits of concepts, such as subroutines, script files, and loops in scripts that form a part of the arsenal of a good Qlik Sense® developer.

*Chapter 4*, *Managing Apps and User Interface*, introduces the user to the concept of publishing Qlik Sense® apps on the server and Qlik Sense® cloud. We will also look at certain key Qlik Sense® objects and their usage for the right purpose and to convey the right information.

*Chapter 5*, *Useful Functions*, deals with some very useful functions available in Qlik Sense®. We present some challenging scenarios that a Qlik Sense® developer faces and provide solutions for these.

*Chapter 6*, *Set Analysis*, is one of the most powerful concepts in Qlik Sense®. This chapter explains to the user the process of writing Set Analysis expressions from scratch. We will also look at some advanced variations in Set Analysis expressions, such as the introduction of flags, defining ranges using the Concat function in Set Analysis expressions, and so on.

*Chapter 7*, *Extensions in Qlik Sense®*, focuses on creating new out-of-the-box extension objects in Qlik Sense® using web technologies.

*Chapter 8*, *What's new in Version 2.1.1?*, discusses the new features introduced in Qlik Sense® version 2.1.1. The users are introduced to the new Qlik Dev Hub and the process to create extension objects using the extension editor and mashups using the mashup editor.

*Appendix*, it gives the details of keyboard shortcuts used in Windows and Mac system.

We also explain how to embed the Qlik Sense® objects on a web page making use of the Single configurator. Some of the other features discussed in the chapter are "Smart Data Profiling"and the new "Smart Search" functionality.

# What you need for this book

The user needs to install Qlik Sense Desktop version 2.1.1, which can be downloaded for free from:

`http://www.qlik.com/try-or-buy/download-qlik-sense`

The user also needs to install Qlik Sense® Server version 2.1.1 for the recipe titled *Publishing a Qlik Sense® application on Qlik Sense® Server,* given in *Chapter 4, Managing Apps and User Interface.*

The Qlik Sense® Server installer file can be obtained from:

`http://www.qlik.com`

One needs to login using the customer account credentials to get access to the files under Support | Customer Downloads.

You also need to install the SAP connector for the recipe titled *Extracting Data from custom Databases* from *Chapter 1, Getting Started with the Data.* In order to work with the SAP connector, you will need to obtain a license from Qlik. A part of this recipe also makes use of QlikView which can be downloaded for free from:

`http://www.qlik.com/try-or-buy/download-qlikview`

# Who this book is for

The book is for anyone who has been exposed to Qlik Sense® and wants to start using it actively for business intelligence. Anybody with a prior knowledge of its sister product, QlikView, will also benefit from this book. Familiarity with the basics of business intelligence is a prerequisite.

# Sections

In this book, you will find several headings that appear frequently (Getting ready, How to do it, How it works, There's more, and See also).

To give clear instructions on how to complete a recipe, we use these sections as follows:

## Getting ready

This section tells you what to expect in the recipe and describes how to set up software or any preliminary settings required for the recipe.

## How to do it...

This section contains the steps required to follow the recipe.

## How it works...

This section usually consists of a detailed explanation of what happened in the previous section.

## There's more...

This section consists of additional information about the recipe in order to make the reader more knowledgeable about the recipe.

## See also

This section provides helpful links to other useful information for the recipe.

# Conventions

In this book, you will find a number of text styles that distinguish between different kinds of information. Here are some examples of these styles and an explanation of their meaning.

Code words in text are shown as follows: "We do this using the INLINE function."

A block of code is set as follows:

```
Sales:
Load * INLINE [
Country, Sales
USA, 6500
UK, 1850
Germany, 3200
];
```

In certain recipes the code is generated on the fly using the Autogenerate function available in Qlik Sense®. In such a case the code will appear as follows:

```
Transactions:
Load
Date(today()-IterNo()) AS Date,
Round(1000*Rand()*Rand()*Rand()) AS Sales
Autogenerate 1000;
```

When we wish to draw your attention to a particular part of a code block, the relevant lines or items are set in bold:

```
Sales:
Load * INLINE [
Country, Sales
USA, 6500
UK, 1850
Germany, 3200
];
```

Any command-line input or output is written as follows:

```
C:\Users\<user>\Documents\Qlik\Sense\Apps
```

**New terms** and **important words** are shown in bold. Words that you see on the screen, for example, in menus or dialog boxes, appear in the text like this: "Click on the **Create New Connection** and select **OLE DB**."

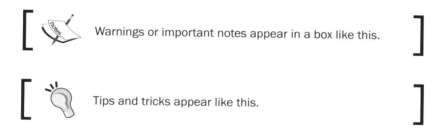

Warnings or important notes appear in a box like this.

Tips and tricks appear like this.

# Reader feedback

Feedback from our readers is always welcome. Let us know what you think about this book—what you liked or disliked. Reader feedback is important for us as it helps us develop titles that you will really get the most out of.

To send us general feedback, simply e-mail feedback@packtpub.com, and mention the book's title in the subject of your message.

If there is a topic that you have expertise in and you are interested in either writing or contributing to a book, see our author guide at www.packtpub.com/authors.

# Customer support

Now that you are the proud owner of a Packt book, we have a number of things to help you to get the most from your purchase.

## Downloading the example code

You can download the example code files from your account at `http://www.packtpub.com` for all the Packt Publishing books you have purchased. If you purchased this book elsewhere, you can visit `http://www.packtpub.com/support` and register to have the files e-mailed directly to you.

## Downloading the color images of this book

We also provide you with a PDF file that has color images of the screenshots/diagrams used in this book. The color images will help you better understand the changes in the output. You can download this file from `http://www.packtpub.com/sites/default/files/downloads/Qlik_Sense_Cookbook.pdf`.

## Errata

Although we have taken every care to ensure the accuracy of our content, mistakes do happen. If you find a mistake in one of our books—maybe a mistake in the text or the code—we would be grateful if you could report this to us. By doing so, you can save other readers from frustration and help us improve subsequent versions of this book. If you find any errata, please report them by visiting `http://www.packtpub.com/submit-errata`, selecting your book, clicking on the **Errata Submission Form** link, and entering the details of your errata. Once your errata are verified, your submission will be accepted and the errata will be uploaded to our website or added to any list of existing errata under the Errata section of that title.

To view the previously submitted errata, go to `https://www.packtpub.com/books/content/support` and enter the name of the book in the search field. The required information will appear under the **Errata** section.

## Piracy

Piracy of copyrighted material on the Internet is an ongoing problem across all media. At Packt, we take the protection of our copyright and licenses very seriously. If you come across any illegal copies of our works in any form on the Internet, please provide us with the location address or website name immediately so that we can pursue a remedy.

Please contact us at `copyright@packtpub.com` with a link to the suspected pirated material.

We appreciate your help in protecting our authors and our ability to bring you valuable content.

## Questions

If you have a problem with any aspect of this book, you can contact us at `questions@packtpub.com`, and we will do our best to address the problem.

# 1

# Getting Started with the Data

In this chapter, we will cover the basic tasks related with extracting data into a Qlik Sense application:

- ▸ Extracting data from databases and data files
- ▸ Extracting data from Web Files
- ▸ Activating the Legacy Mode in Qlik Sense® desktop
- ▸ Extracting data from custom databases
- ▸ Invoking help while in the data load editor or the expression editor
- ▸ Previewing data in the Data model viewer
- ▸ Creating a Master Library from the Data model viewer
- ▸ Using a Master Library in the Edit mode

## Introduction

Data is the core aspect of any Business Intelligence application. It provides information that helps organizations to make decisions.

A Qlik Sense application is based on the data extracted from various sources, such as relational databases, CRM systems, ERP systems, and data files.

This chapter introduces the user to various methods of extracting data into a Qlik Sense application effectively. It is assumed that the reader is already acquainted with the concepts of ODBC, OLEDB, and relational databases. The chapter also provides an essential recipe for fetching the data into Qlik Sense from a SAP system. The SAP connector can be downloaded from the Qlik website and installed before working on the recipe. You need to acquire a valid license enabler file beforehand, in order to download the SAP connector.

The later part of the chapter focuses on a few recipes regarding the creation of a library and content.

# Extracting data from databases and data files

The data within an organization is usually stored in relational databases and data files. Extracting data is the first step towards creating a data model. The following section demonstrates the steps to extract data from an MS Access database and a delimited (.CSV) file. The procedure to extract data from other relational databases is the same as the process for extracting data from MS Access.

The dataset that we will use is available publicly and covers information about routes and fares of various transport systems in Hong Kong. The original data files have been downloaded from (https://data.gov.hk/) website. This dataset can also be obtained from the Packt Publishing website.

The data connections in the Qlik Sense data load editor save shortcuts leading to commonly used data sources, such as databases and data files. The following types of connections exist in Qlik Sense:

- ▶ ODBC database connection
- ▶ OLEDB database connection
- ▶ Folder connection
- ▶ Web file connection

This recipe deals with the ODBC, OLEDB, and Folder connections. The web file connection will be dealt with in a separate recipe.

## Getting ready...

The dataset required for this recipe that is downloaded from the Packt Publishing website comes in a zipped folder called as QlikSenseData. Extract all the files from this zipped folder and save them on the hard drive at a desired location.

If you are connecting to the database using **Open Database Connectivity** (**ODBC**) then:

1. Install the relevant ODBC drivers on your system.

 For the sake of our exercise, we need the MS Access drivers. The system DSN connection can be set up through the ODBC administrator under the **Administrative Tools** in **Control Panel**.

2. While setting up the ODBC connection, select the ROUTE_BUS.mdb file as the Data Source from the QlikSenseData folder.

3. Name the ODBC DSN connection as HongKong Buses.

4. Create a new Qlik Sense application and open the data load editor.

5. Click on the **Create New Connection** and select **ODBC**.

6. Select **HongKong Buses** under **System DSN**.

7. Name the data connection as Qlik Sense CookBook ODBC.

8. The following image shows the details we enter in the **Create new connection (ODBC)** window:

If you are connecting to the database using OLE DB connectivity, we can directly set this up through the editor:

1. Open the data load editor in Qlik Sense.

2. Click on the **Create New Connection** and select **OLE DB**.

3. Select the **Microsoft Jet 4.0 OLE DB Provider (32 Bit)** driver from the provider drop-down list.

4. Insert the **Data Source** file path, which in our case will be the path for the ROUTE_BUS.mdb file in the QlikSenseData folder.

5. Name the data connection as QlikSense CookBook OLE DB.

6. The following image shows the details we enter in the **Create new connection (OLE DB)** window:

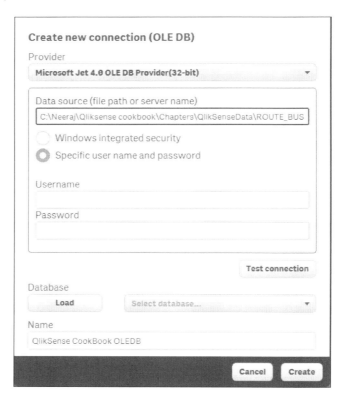

If you are extracting the data from a data file, such as `.CSV`, perform the following steps:

1. Open the data load editor in Qlik Sense.
2. Click on **Create New Connection** and select **Folder**.
3. Select the location of the `QlikSenseData` folder which contains our data files. Alternatively, one can directly enter the path of the source folder under **Path**.
4. Name the data connection as `Qlik Sense CookBook Data`.
5. The following image shows the details we enter in the **Create new connection (folder)** window:

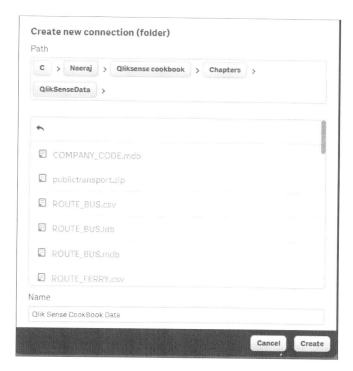

6. Once the connections are created in the Qlik Sense library, they will be seen as a list under **Data connections** in the data load editor, as shown in the following screenshot:

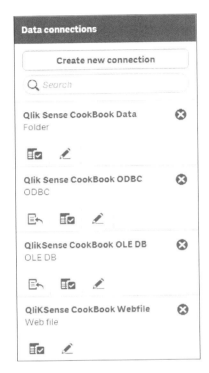

## How to do it...

If you are working with an ODBC or an OLEDB data connection, follow the steps:

1. Insert the relevant data connection string to the script by clicking on **Insert connection string,** as shown in the following screenshot:

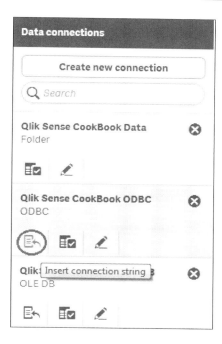

2. Next, click on **Select data** under **Data connections** to view and extract data from the
   ROUTE table in the MS Access database, as shown:

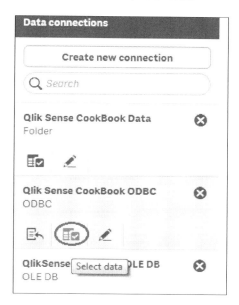

3. The preview of the ROUTE_BUS.mdb table will look like the following. The fields in the table can be excluded or renamed while working in the **Preview** window, as shown in the following screenshot:

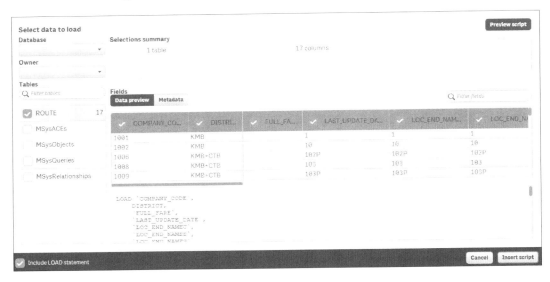

4. Click on **Insert Script** in the **Preview** window. This will insert the connection string as well as load the statement to the script. Make sure that you delete the duplicate LIB CONNECT TO 'Qlik Sense CookBook ODBC'; statement from your script.

5. Load the data in your application by clicking on the Load data button.

Keep the **Close when successfully finished** option checked in the data load progress window. If the data is loaded successfully, then the window automatically closes or else the error encountered is highlighted.

1. On a similar note, in order to test the Qlik Sense data files, Click on the **Select data** option under the **Qlik Sense CookBook Data** connection.

2. Next, select the ROUTE_GMB.csv file from the QlikSenseData folder and load it in the application.

3. The preview of the ROUTE_GMB.csv table will look like the following screenshot. Make sure that you select **Embedded field names** under **Field names**. Note that the **Delimiter** in this case is automatically set to **Comma**.

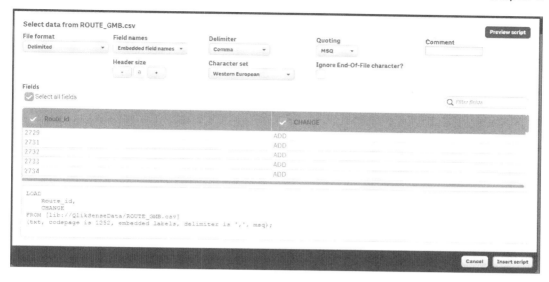

4. Insert the script and then save and load it.

## How it works...

The `LIB CONNECT TO` statement connects to a database using a stored data connection from the Qlik Sense library; thus, acting as a bridge between our application and the data source.

## There's more...

This recipe aimed at extracting data from common data sources, such as RDBMSs and data files. Qlik Sense can also extract data from web files and custom data sources such as SAP. We will see this in the forthcoming section.

## See also...

► *Creating a Master Library from the Data model viewer*

# Extracting data from Web Files

Often, the data required for the purpose of reporting is not stored in a database, but instead needs to be fetched from a website. For example, customer location information specifically the geographic co-ordinates used in mapping analysis is not available internally within an organization. This information may be available on the web and can be extracted from there.

## Getting ready...

When extracting the data from a web file:

1. Open an existing Qlik Sense application or create a new one.

2. Open the data load editor.

3. Click on **Create New Connection** and select **Web** file.

4. The **Select web file** window will open.

5. Insert the following URL from which you can fetch the data:

   `http://www.csgnetwork.com/llinfotable.html`

6. Name the connection as `QlikSense Cookbook Webfile`, as shown:

## How to do it...

1. In the list under **Data Connections**, select **QlikSense Cookbook Webfile** and click on **Select Data**. This will open up a preview window listing out all the tables from the web page. When you carefully examine the table contents, you realize that it is the second table **@2** that contains the location information.

2. Check the box next to **@2** and ensure that it is selected, so the correct table is shown in the preview. The user will need to change the value under **Field names** to **embedded field names**.

3. The preview of the table will look like the following screenshot:

4. Select all the fields from the table in the preview window. Click on **Insert script** to load the web data in the application.

5. Name the table as `Country_Location` and the script will read as follows:

```
Country_Location:
LOAD
Country,
Capital,
Latitude,
Longitude
FROM [lib://QlikSense Cookbook Webfile]
(html, codepage is 1252, embedded labels, table is @2);
```

6. Save and load the data. Once the script is successfully loaded, the data model viewer will show the loaded table.

## How it works...

Qlik Sense connects to the web file using the stored data connection. Once connected it identifies the tables in the HTML source and lists them in the preview window.

Certain external websites require authentication in order to be accessed and Qlik Sense is unable to cope with websites that are secured in this manner. In order to get over this issue, we can use a third party data extraction tool. The extracted data can be stored in a data file, such as a **qvd**. The qvd file can then be used as a data source in the Qlik Sense application.

## There's more...

Qlik Sense can also extract data from other data formats, such as XML. The underlying principles remain the same as explained in the preceding recipes.

## See also...

> ▶ *Creating a Master Library from the Data model viewer*
> ▶ *Activating the Legacy Mode in Qlik Sense® desktop*

# Activating the Legacy Mode in Qlik Sense® desktop

Qlik Sense is a developing product; hence, certain features are not active when running the Desktop version in its standard mode. A prime example of this is using the `Custom Connect to` statement to create the ODBC/OLEDB connection strings or attempting to connect to a custom database as SAP. Both these activities are not possible if Qlik Sense runs in its standard mode. In order to get these functionalities to run, we need to activate the legacy mode. However, one must note that enabling the legacy mode has security implications, if the application is deployed on the Sense server then one does not have control over the data connections in QMC (if the legacy mode is activated). The library security features may also be lost; moreover, the legacy mode does not work with Qlik Cloud either.

## Getting ready...

Activating the Legacy Mode requires changing a parameter value in the `settings.ini` file for Qlik Sense.

## How to do it...

1. Make sure that Qlik Sense Desktop is closed before opening the `settings.ini` file.
2. Open the `settings.ini` file that is by default stored under `C:\Users\{user}\Documents\Qlik\Sense\Settings.ini`.
3. Change `StandardReload=1` to `StandardReload=0`.
4. Save the file and start Qlik Sense Desktop in order to run it in a legacy mode, as shown:

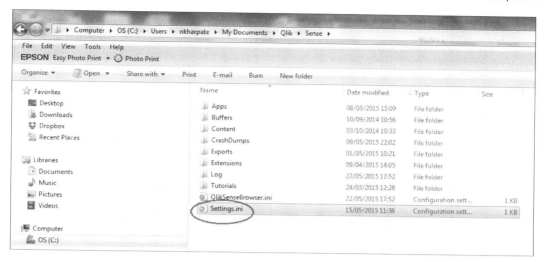

## How it works...

Changing the value for the `StandardReload` parameter in the `settings.ini` file enables the Legacy Mode in Qlik Sense. When running in the Legacy mode, any of the scripts in Qlik View can be directly used in Qlik Sense. This will also allow us to use the library connections.

## There's more...

The Qlik Sense has the capability to use the same script that is found in any Qlikview file. One can also use a binary load statement in Qlik Sense in order to load the entire data model from an existing Qlikview file. All the `Custom Connect To` statements can only be used after we activate the legacy mode.

## See also...

►   *Extracting data from custom databases*

# Extracting data from custom databases

The current version of Qlik Sense does not support the loading of data from custom databases, such as SAP or Salesforce. Nevertheless, it can still be achieved in a few simple steps. The following recipe explains the steps to load data from a SAP database.

## Getting ready...

The **Custom connector** option under **Create new connection** is not available in the Qlik Sense data load editor. This feature is going to be introduced soon in a forthcoming release of the product.

The following recipe requires you to use another Qlik product named **Qlikview** in order to generate the extract script that is to be copied and used in the Qlik Sense application. Qlikview is free software that can be downloaded from the Qlik website. The recipe also requires the **SAP connector** for QlikView to be installed.

## How to do it...

Once we install the SAP connector, the `RELOADSAPDD.qvw` and `ScriptBuilder.qvw` files are saved on the hard drive.

We will work along with the `RELOADSAPDD.qvw` file, which is stored at the `C:\ProgramData\QlikTech\CustomData\QvSAPConnector\ScriptBuilder` location.

In order to extract data from a custom database, such as SAP:

1. Activate the legacy mode as described in the recipe just prior to this.

2. Open the Qlikview file and input the SAP credentials to generate the connection string similar to the following:
   ```
   CUSTOM CONNECT TO ""Provider=QvSAPConnector.dll;
   ASHOST=192.168.210.166;SYSNR=00;CLIENT=100;KeepCasing=1;
   NullDate=1;XUserId=UPJDRIRJJaSMVEVIXSFA;XPassword=
   IQWOQIRNJbaMXUVMXLMGSEA;"";
   ```

3. Open Qlik Sense. Copy and paste the SAP Connection string from the script editor of the QlikView file to Qlik Sense.

4. Similarly, one can copy and paste the load script generated for any SAP table in a QlikView file to a Qlik Sense file.

5. Save and load data.

6. The data load editor with all the connection strings will appear, as shown in the following:

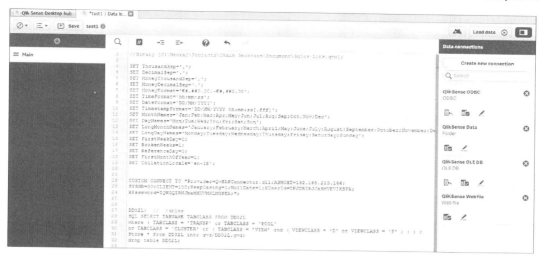

## How it works...

The essence of the recipe is that the custom connections don't work in Qlik Sense, unless it is running in a Legacy mode. The user can copy the script generated in the QlikView file to the Qlik Sense Load script while running the application in the legacy mode, as this script cannot be generated directly in Qlik Sense.

## There's more...

Qlik Sense can extract data from any data source that can be loaded by QlikView (such as Salesforce) in practically the same way as it is described in this recipe.

## See also...

▸ Activating the Legacy Mode in Qlik Sense® desktop

# Invoking help while in the data load editor or the expression editor

As a Qlik Sense developer, one often needs access to the help module in order to search for certain functions or simply understand their usage and syntax in detail. Help is available in the dropdown menu on the toolbar. However, when we use this option, it takes us to www. help.qlik.com/sense and then we again need to search for the keyword. It's not a huge effort but it would be more beneficial if we were taken directly to the information regarding the keyword or function we are looking for.

## Getting ready...

For this recipe, we will use the `Automotive.qvf` file, which comes as a built in example when we install the Qlik Sense Desktop.

## How to do it...

1.  Open the `Automotive.qvf` file from the Qlik Sense desktop hub.
2.  Open the data load editor and go to the **Territory data** tab.
3.  Click the **Help** ( ? ) button inside the data load editor. This will highlight the script so that all the keywords are then clickable links.
4.  Click on the keyword `pick` in the script. This will take us to the correct place in the help file, as shown:

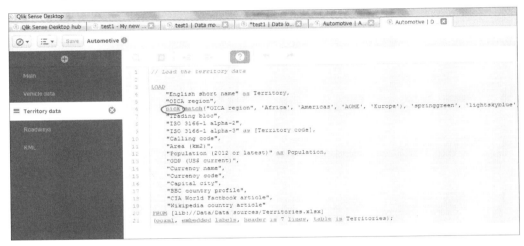

## There's more...

An alternative approach that can be used in Qlik Sense versions prior to 2.0.1 is as follows:

1.  Highlight the key word `pick` in the script.
2.  Press *ctrl + h*. This will take you directly to the content explaining **Pick** on the help page.

A list of useful shortcuts for Qlik Sense is given at the end of this book.

## See also...

►   Keyboard shortcuts in Qlik Sense® desktop

# Previewing data in the Data model viewer

As any experienced Qlik developer will tell you, the data model viewer is a key component you will undoubtedly spend time using on your Qlik journey. Qlik Sense has brought with it some nice new features. We will also delve into the different insights that can be gleaned from the data model viewer:

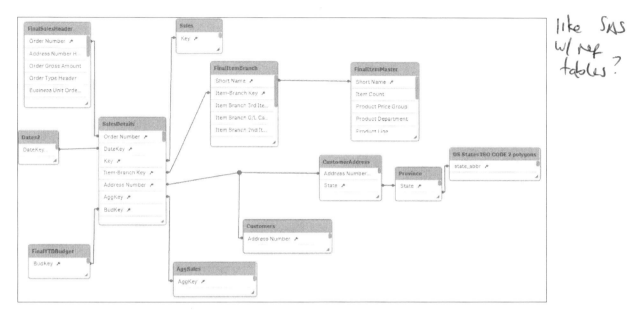

*like SAS w/ ref tables?*

## Getting ready

For this recipe, we will make use of the Data model viewer.qvf application. This file is available for download on the Packt Publishing website.

## How to do it...

1. Open the Data model viewer.qvf application that has been downloaded from the resource library.
2. Click on data model viewer in the Navigation dropdown on the toolbar.

## How it works...

In this section we will see how the different types of data are viewed.

## Viewing the data model

The data model consists of a number of tables joined by the key fields. The following screenshot contains functions that can be used to manipulate the layout of the data model:

The detail of the available keys (from right to left) is given as follows:

- **Collapse all**: This reduces down the tables to just their headers; thus, hiding all the fields
- **Show linked fields**: Expands the tables enough to only display the key fields in each
- **Expand all**: Displays all the fields for each table
- **Internal Table viewer**: Shows the internal representation of the data model
- **Layout**: Provides options to auto align the table grid or space out across the screen
- **Preview**: Toggles the data preview screen to either on or off

## Viewing the associations

Clicking on a table will highlight its associated tables in orange. The customer's table is selected in the following screenshot and the shared key here is **Address Number**:

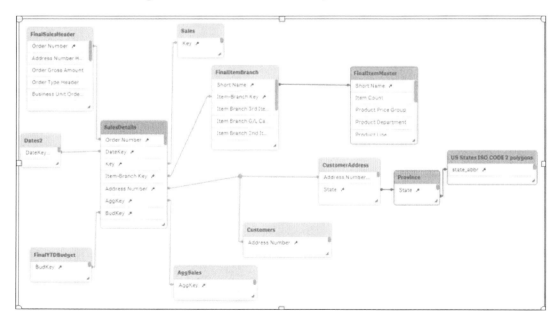

Click on the **CustomerAddress** table to see a highlighted expansion, via the state key, as shown:

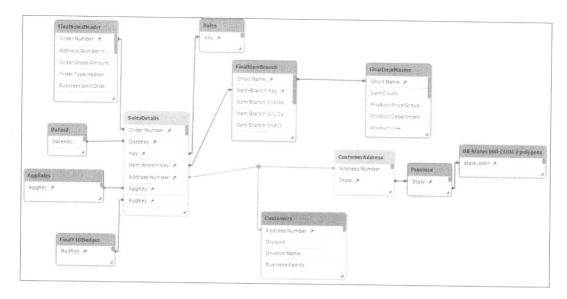

## Table Meta Data

The data model viewer also provides information on the contents of each table.

Click the header of the customer address table then open the **Preview** pane by clicking the **Preview** button in the bottom left hand corner.

The following preview will be displayed at the bottom of the screen:

Along with a small snippet of the table contents, the far left table also provides some high level table information about the number of rows, fields, keys as well as any tags.

Next, click the **Address Number** field from the Customers table in the data model viewer.

You can now see more detailed information about the individual field.

These are:

- ▸ Density
- ▸ Subset ratio
- ▸ Has duplicates
- ▸ Total distinct values
- ▸ Present distinct values non-null values
- ▸ Tags

This information is very helpful when we are debugging issues. If a count does not return the expected result, you may want to ensure that there are no duplicates.

If a selection is not filtered correctly you may want to check the sub-set ratio of the key and so on.

## There's more...

Double clicking a table header in the data model viewer will either collapse or expand the table fully.

# Creating a Master Library from the Data model viewer

To help reduce the repetition and developer error, Qlik has introduced a master library where we can store reusable items, such as dimensions, measures and even whole visualizations. For people experienced in Qlik's other products such as QlikView, just think; "no more linked objects and storing expressions in variables!"

It is easy to think of library items in a self-service context. Don't get me wrong; ultimately you will have to decide what will be published; from your data model to the world for their own analysis purposes. Having said that, the secret sauce of this recipe is in saving your own time.

It is a productivity hack that implies; "automation is to your time what compound interest is to money". While it is not an exact parallel, this is a nice concept to frame the usefulness of timesaving functions in Qlik Sense. The effective use of the library saves time spent on scrolling down field lists, rewriting expressions over and over, applying a single change in multiple places, and so on.

Once you have saved enough time to eclipse the setup investment, the value of taking this approach can only compound with continuous development.

# Getting ready

1. Create a new Qlik Sense application and name it `Master Library`.

2. Open the data load editor.

3. Enter the following script and load the data by clicking on the `Load data ⊙` button. (The script is available in a separate text file that can be downloaded from the Packt Publishing website):

```
Data:
LOAD * INLINE [
    Name, Region, Country, City, OrderId, Sales, Company,
    OrderDate
    Wooten, C, Mozambique, Carmen, 1, 45.55, Est Nunc
    Laoreet LLC, 22/12/14
    Blankenship, Delta, Cayman Islands, Sapele, 2, 95.76,
    Lorem Donec Inc., 17/01/15
    Sheppard, Wyoming, Vatican City State, Cheyenne, 3,
    38.31, Lobortis, 07/08/14
    Goddard, H, Curaçao, San Francisco, 4, 86.33, Non Inc.,
    07/09/14
    Galloway, Aragón, Trinidad & Tobago, Zaragoza, 5,
    85.80, Diam Proin., 21/01/15
    Kirsten, Tamil Nadu, Wallis & Futuna, Neyveli, 6,
    28.47, Mollis Non Limited, 03/05/14
    Holland, Cartago, Falkland Islands, San Diego, 7, 1.34,
    Ullamcorper Inc., 17/07/14
    Thaddeus, BC, Canada, Oliver, 8, 59.04, Ante Nunc
    Mauris Ltd, 17/02/15
    Lareina, CA, Spain, San Diego, 9, 4.55, Pellentesque
    Tincidunt Limited, 29/07/14
    Jescie, Vienna, Monaco, Vienna, 10, 54.20, Ultricies
    Ligula Consulting, 16/06/14
    Logan, IL, Saint Barthélemy, Paris, 11, 91.31, Mi
    Foundation, 13/12/14
    Shannon, CG, Nepal, Aberystwyth, 12, 80.86, Auctor Non
    LLC, 03/05/14
    Andrew, SO, Argentina, Sokoto, 13, 88.78, Scelerisque
    Mollis Associates, 12/12/14
    Jocelyn, WP, Tanzania, Konin, 14, 15.91, Ligula Tortor
    Dictum Ltd, 22/08/14
    Gordon, FL, Hong Kong, Miami, 15, 93.97, Suscipit Inc.,
    12/05/14
];
```

## How to do it...

Once the data has been loaded, you can check the results by opening the data model viewer through the navigation dropdown ( ⊘▾ ) in the top corner on the left hand side of the toolbar, as shown in the following screenshot:

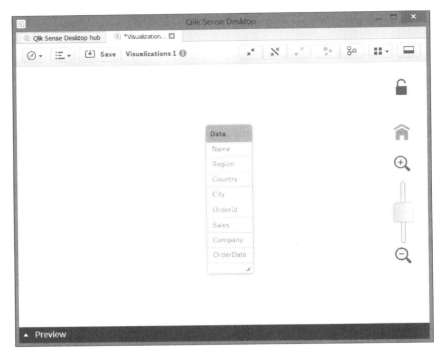

You can find the **Preview** button to the bottom left of the screen. There are several other places in Qlik Sense where you can create master library items but the data model preview screen is the best, as it also lets you see the data first. Take a minute to browse the data you have loaded in data model viewer.

1. In the data model viewer, select the Data table by clicking on its header and then click the **Preview** button to view the fields and the field values loaded from the Data table.

2. The **Preview** window will appear as shown in the following:

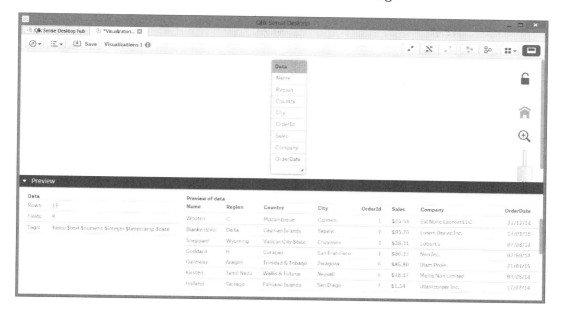

3. Select the **Region** field from the table to get the preview as shown in the following:

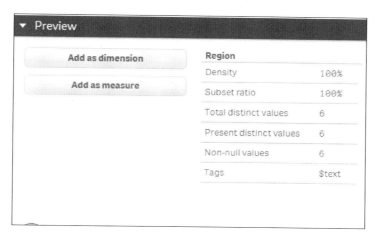

4. Next, click the **Add as dimension** button.

5.   The following window appears. If you are likely to publish this dimension for consumption by users, you can enter a description here:

6.   It is advised to use tags to make our life easier. Add the tag **Geo** and click on ⊕ .

7.   Now click on    **Add dimension**    to create a Master dimension in the library.

8.   Repeat this process for the **Country** and **City** fields.

9.   Click on **Done** to go back to the data model viewer.

10. Finally, it's time to create a measure. Select the **Sales** field from the `Data` table in the data model viewer.

11. Click the [Add as measure] button. When we create a Master measure we need to make sure we use an aggregation function such as `Sum`, `Avg`, and so on, along with the selected field.

12. In the **Create new measure** window, type `SUM` in front of (**Sales**), as shown in the following image:

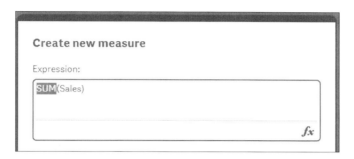

13. Click on **Create**.

14. Save the changes made in the master library by clicking on the [Save] button on the toolbar in the table preview. Exit the table preview by going to the App Overview.

15. Open (or create) a sheet and enter the edit mode by clicking on the [✏ Edit] button.

16. Once you are in the edit mode, click the chain ( 🔗 ) icon on the left hand side of the asset panel to open the Master items menu.

17. To add visualizations, first create them in the user interface then drag them into the library.

While the Master item menu panel is very useful to speed up the development when defining the contents, it is easier to do it from the filters pane. In short, you can browse the entire contents of your data model and right-click on the most important fields to add the ones that will be frequently used.

## How it works...

1. Right click on a field from the field's pane that you want to add to the master library.

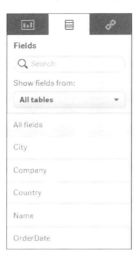

2. Click on **Create Dimension**, enter a **Description** and any relevant **Tags**, click **Done** once finished:

## There's more...

We can also create Master dimensions and measures through the GUI. In order to do this:

1. Open an existing sheet or create a new one.
2. Click on the Master items 🔗 icon.
3. Click on either Dimensions or Measures. This will enable an option to create new library items.

# Using a Master Library in the Edit mode

As mentioned in the previous recipe, a great benefit of creating a master library is to save you time and reduce the complexity by applying global changes to your visualizations.

There are three main areas in the asset panel when editing a Qlik Sense sheet (Objects, Fields, and Master items). Clicking the 🔗 chain button opens the Master items pane.

From here, you can manage every aspect of the Master items, such as renaming, replacing, deleting, and editing.

## Getting ready

You can continue to use the application from the previous recipe.

1. If you have not completed the previous recipe. Load the following in your data load editor:

```
LOAD * INLINE [
Country, Area, Sales
USA, North, 1000
USA, North, 1200
USA, South, 2500
USA, South, 2500
UK, North, 1000
UK, North, 2500
UK, South, 2000
UK, South, 1900
];
```

2. Add **Country** and **Area** as Master dimensions both with the tag **Geo**.
3. Add **Sales** as a Master measure.

## How to do it...

1. Open the **App overview** screen by clicking on the navigation dropdown on the toolbar at the top.

2. Create a new sheet or open an existing one.

3. Enter the edit mode by clicking on the ✏ **Edit** button.

4. Click on the object pane button ▮▮▮ and double click on the bar chart button. ▮▮▮ Bar chart .The chart will be added to the main content area automatically.

5. Type Geo in the search box of the asset panel on the left of your screen. While there are no charts called **Geo**, the search has flagged up our two tagged dimensions in the master library pane with a yellow circle like this ▮▮ ▤ ⦿ .

6. Next, drag the **Area** field to where it says **Add dimension**. Repeat the steps where the **Country** field selects **Add "Country"** when prompted, as shown:

7. Clear your search on Geo by pressing the ⊗ button.

8. Click on **Measures**.

9. Drag the **Sales** measure from the asset panel over to the add measure area of the chart. Voila! You have created your first visualization using Master dimensions and measures:

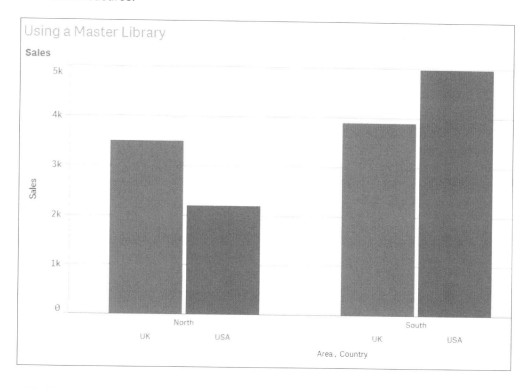

10. You can now drag this chart into the asset panel and it will become a master visualization.

## There's more...

If you delete a Master dimension or Master measure, the visualizations that use the deleted Master item will not work unless you replace it with a new dimension or measure. The same applies to deleting a field from the data model; the reference will remain a part of the Master item pane until it's updated from the edit screen.

Echoing a comment in the previous chapter regarding time saving and creating Master measures, replaces the need to write expressions as variables for reuse. Another piece of QlikView functionality that has been replicated and expanded upon is the concept of linked objects. Any updates you make in the Master visualization area will be applied globally.

If you rename a field in your script without moving the position it will be applied automatically to all the objects.

# 2
# Visualizations

In this chapter, we will cover some visualization tips and tricks to create a compelling dashboard in Qlik Sense:

- Creating Snapshots
- Creating and adding content to a story
- Adding embedded sheets to the story
- Highlighting the performance measure in a bar chart
- Associating persistent colors to field values
- Using the `colormix1` function
- Composition
- Relationships
- Comparison
- Distribution
- Structuring visualizations

## Introduction

A typical Qlik Sense application should always follow the **Dashboard Analysis Reporting** (**DAR**) methodology. This methodology focuses on developing a Dashboard sheet followed by an analysis sheet and then a reports sheet. The Dashboard projects the high-level figures of the business; the analysis sheet gives more control to the end user to filter the data, while the Reports sheet has the detailed information at a granular level. For more information on the DAR concept, visit:

- `https://community.qlik.com/blogs/qlikviewdesignblog/2013/11/08/dar-methodology`

While this concept can be easily implemented within the application, one often tends to forget the best design practices that help in making the applications more engaging for the users. An optimal design will convey the right information to the right people at the right time. This will elevate the decision making process within the organization.

The following chapter focuses on some of the key concepts in data visualization that will help the users take their Qlik Sense design capabilities to the next level.

It also discusses the importance of choosing the right visualization for the right purpose. Some useful blogs written by the experts in data visualization can be accessed by the users to enhance their knowledge:

▶ `http://www.perceptualedge.com/blog/`

▶ `http://global.qlik.com/uk/blog/authors/patrik-lundblad`

# Creating Snapshots

Snapshots are an exciting feature in Qlik Sense that enables the users to capture the point in time state of the data object. Snapshots work as insights for a story which will be discussed in later recipes.

## Getting ready

For the sake of this exercise, we will make use of the `Automotive.qvf` Qlik Sense application. This application is downloaded as a sample file with the default Qlik Sense desktop installation and can be accessed through the Qlik Sense hub.

The sample files may differ by region. If the `Automotive.qvf` application is not available in the Qlik Sense hub, it can be downloaded from the Packt Publishing website.

Perform the following steps once you download the application from the Packt Publishing website:

1. Copy the `.qvf` file to `C:\Users\<user>\Documents\Qlik\Sense\Apps` `folder`.
2. Open Qlik Sense desktop and the app will appear in the hub.

## How to do it...

Qlik Sense provides you the opportunity to take a single snapshot of a selected object or take several snapshots of multiple objects at the same time.

In order to take Snapshots,

1. Open the `Automotive.qvf` application from the Qlik Sense hub:

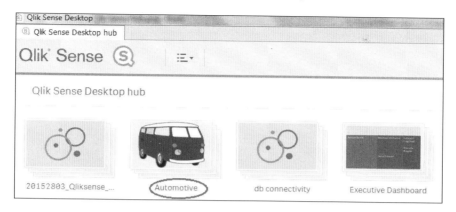

2. Open the **Sales Overview** sheet and select the trendline chart **Vehicle Sales by year**. Right-click on the object to display the options and select 📷 to take a snapshot.

3. The snapshot is saved within the snapshot library and is titled with the same name as the object.

In order to take multiple snapshots at the same time, use the following steps:

1. While you are still in the sheet view, click 📷 on the toolbar. The objects for which we can take snapshots are marked in broken orange lines, as shown:

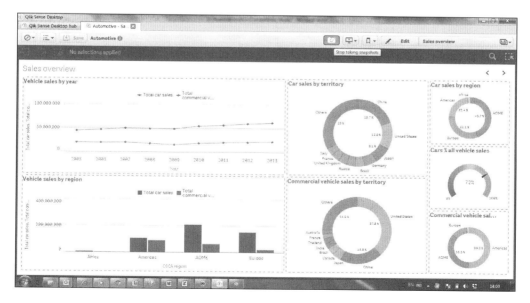

2. Next, click on any object whose snapshot you want to take. As we click around on the sheet objects, a snapshot gets saved in the library automatically and a snapshot image 📷 is displayed at the top right corner for every individual object along with the count of snapshots attached to the object.

3. For our exercise, we will save snapshots for **Car Sales by Industry** and **Vehicle sales by Region**.

4. As mentioned, the snapshots are again saved within the snapshot library and are titled with the same name as the objects.

## How it works...

Snapshots are usually taken by the users when they want to store the point-in-time picture of an object corresponding to any selections. Snapshots are synonymous with taking a static picture of the object on the screen. As this is a static picture, it does not get updated with the change in data or with the change in state of the individual Qlik Sense object. The state and selections within a snapshot will not be updated after a data reload.

A Snapshot can be called a sibling of another Qlik Sense feature called **Bookmarks**. The difference being, Bookmarks capture the state of selections within an application, while Snapshots store the state of objects as it was at a particular point of time. The data projected by a bookmark gets updated on data reload.

## There's more...

Snapshots form the basis of creating stories in Qlik Sense. We deal with stories in the following sections.

## See also

▶ *Creating and adding content to a story*

# Creating and adding content to a story

Qlik Sense introduces the concept of storytelling within the application. The data story interface helps the user to collate all the important observations and insights from the application to create a convincing narrative and present it to the intended audience in the form of a slideshow.

## Getting ready

As in the previous recipe, we will again make use of the `Automotive.qvf`
Qlik Sense application.

## How to do it...

To create a story, perform the following steps:

1. Open the `Automotive.qvf` application.

2. While you are still on the **App overview** page, click ⬚ **Stories** on the toolbar.

3. Click on the ⊕ sign to create new story.

4. Add the story name as `Sales Overview` and description as `A narrative of the overall sales for the company.`

5. Click outside the description window to save the story.

Adding contents to a storyboard:

1. Open the storyboard for "Sales Overview" by clicking on the thumbnail.

2. The right side pane of the storyboard represents five libraries which serve as the source for the contents which we can use for our storyline:

3. Click on the **Snapshot library** icon. This will display the list of snapshots we took in the earlier recipe:

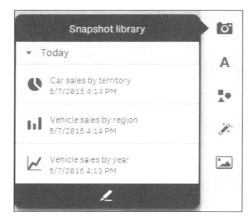

4. Drag and drop the **Vehicle sales by region** and **Car sales by territory** snapshot on the sheet.

5. Click on the **Text Library**. Drag and drop the **Title** box on the sheet.

6. Double click the **Title** box and add the title Sales by Region and Territory.

7. Click on the **Text Library**. Drag and drop the **Paragraph** box on the sheet.

8. Double click on the Paragraph box and add the following text:

   ❑ AOME region has the highest number of total car sales while if we consider commercial vehicles, Americas leads the way.

   ❑ China is the biggest market for cars followed by United States. There is very little comparison amongst the volume of sales for european nations Italy France and United Kingdom.

9. Click on the **Shapes** library. Drag and drop the ◀ and ▼ shapes on the sheet.

10. Save the story by clicking on Save on the toolbar.

11. The effective story interface should look like this:

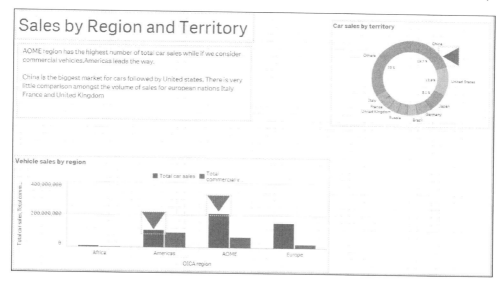

12. The story can be played as a presentation by clicking on the 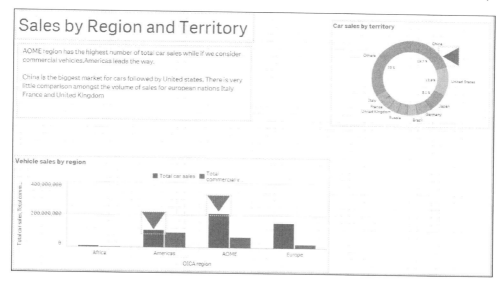 button on the left-hand side vertical pane.

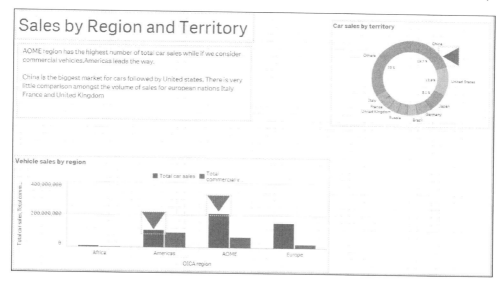 How it works...

The story with all the essential elements, namely the snapshots, commentary and the highlighters, conveys the essence of the data to the audience. The data added through the snapshots contains static point in time information. Since stories are native to Qlik Sense, there is no need to create separate PowerPoint files for presentations. Although with Qlik Sense version 2.1.1, one has the option to export the stories to PowerPoint so that they can be shared offline.

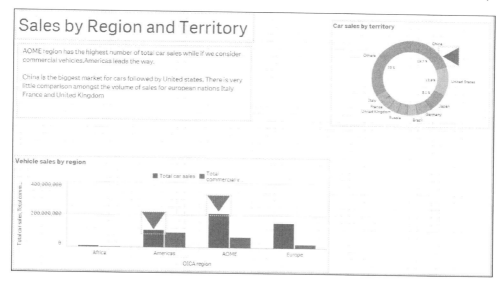 There's more...

While working in the story Edit mode, click on any individual object. On clicking the object we will find two options highlighted on the top right-hand corner. The first one is 📷 for **Replace snapshot** and the other one is 🔒 for **Unlock the snapshot**. Use the following steps to explore the **Replace snapshot** and **Unlock the snapshot** functionalities:

1. Click on **Replace snapshot**.

2. The following dropdown appears which lists all the snapshots captured for the original visualization. The snapshot in use is marked with a ✓ :

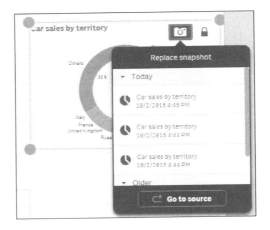

3. The user can replace the existing snapshot with a new one.

4. Alternatively, the user can click on the **⇄ Go to source** button in the dropdown that opens the original sheet where the visualization resides. New snapshots can then be created using the live data.

5. Click on **⇄ Return** button on the original sheet to return to the story.

6. Next, click on the 🔒 button for visualization. This will unlock the snapshot and activate the edit 🖉 option.

7. Click on 🖉 to change the basic properties of the object. The modified properties for the object are specific to the story. The object on the Qlik Sense sheet still has the original properties, as shown:

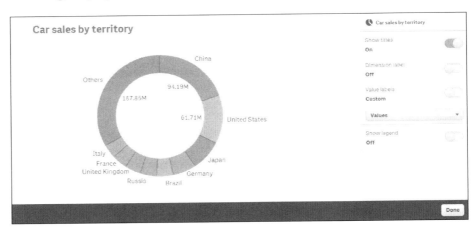

A Qlik Sense storyline can also have embedded sheets. This is particularly useful if we want to showcase the entire content of the sheet on the slide.

## See also

▸ *Adding embedded sheets to the story*

# Adding embedded sheets to the story

Multiple sheets can be added to the story and the following section deals with the steps involved.

## Getting ready

As in the previous recipe, we will again make use of the `Automotive.qvf` Qlik Sense application:

1. Open the `Automotive.qvf` application from the Qlik Sense hub.
2. Next, open the **Sales Overview** story, which was created in the previous recipe by clicking 🖵 **Stories** on the toolbar.

## How to do it...

1. In the story view, click on the ⊕ image at the bottom left corner of the storyboard.
2. Select either **Sheet left-aligned** or **Sheet** from the **Add slide** pop up:

3. A slide with a sheet placeholder is added to the screen. Next, click on **Select Sheet** and select the **In-use overview** sheet from the dialog box, as shown in the following screenshot:

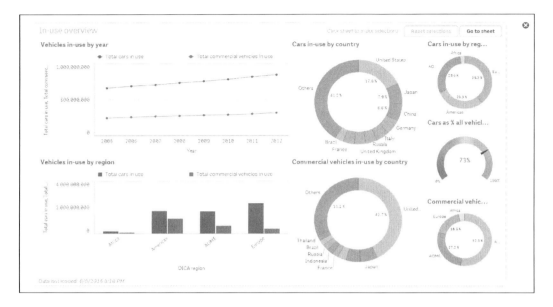

4. Save the file by clicking on the `Save` button.

5. The story can be played as a presentation by clicking on the ▶ button on the left-hand side vertical pane.

## How it works...

When we embed a sheet into our story, it places all the contents of the desired sheet on the slide. The embedded sheet always has the same set of selections as the sheet in the sheet view.

## There's more...

When we play the story, you will observe that we have two buttons at the top of the embedded sheet slide, namely `Reset selections` and `Go to sheet`. Selections can be made on the embedded sheet by clicking on each individual object. The `Reset selections` button clears the selections and the `Go to sheet` option takes the user back to the original sheet where new snapshots of objects can be taken. The `Go to sheet` button is also available in the edit-mode of the embedded sheet.

We can add effects and images to the story using the **Effects** and **Media library**, which is available in the storytelling view.

# Highlighting the performance measure in a bar chart

One of the essential components of a Qlik Sense dashboard is the **Key Performance Indicators** or the **KPIs**. The KPIs indicate the health of the company based on specific measures. The information displayed in the KPI should stand out distinctly and demand attention. For example, one of the key KPIs that a CEO of the company may like to have on his dashboard is "Actuals vs Budget". A CEO is mostly interested in knowing if the company is below or above the budgeted figures. So, it makes sense to highlight the required information inside the visualization object. The following recipe explains and shows you how to do this in a bar chart.

## Getting ready

A "Dial Gauge" is quite commonly used to display the key KPIs in Qlik Sense. However, the best design practices say that the "Bar chart" is the most effective way of conveying the information to the user. The following example makes use of a bar chart to strengthen this thought.

Perform the following steps to get started:

1. Create a new Qlik Sense application. Name it `Performance Measure_Bar Chart`.
2. Open the data load editor.
3. Load the following script, which contains information on the `Actuals` and `Budget` for four products. The script can be downloaded from the Packt Publishing website:

```
Products:
LOAD * INLINE [
Product, Actuals, Budget
Footwear, 100000, 120000
Tyres, 180000, 150000
Mountain Bikes, 250000, 195000
Road Bikes, 200000, 225000
];
```

## How to do it...

The following steps highlight the performance measure in a bar chart:

1. Open the **App overview** and create a new sheet.
2. Create a bar chart on the sheet.
3. Add **Product** as the first dimension.

4. Under the Properties panel present on the right-hand side. Click on the **Add data ▾** dropdown menu and select **Dimension**.

5. Open the expression editor by clicking on *fx* .

6. Add the following calculation as the second dimension and name it as `Performance Type`:

```
=ValueList ('Actuals Up To Budget','Actuals Below
  Budget','Actuals Above Budget')
```

7. Click on **Add data ▾** again and add the following measure to the object and call it as `Performance`:

```
if(ValueList ('Actuals Up To Budget','Actuals Below
  Budget','Actuals Above Budget')='Actuals Up To Budget',
  RangeMin(Sum(Budget),Sum(Actuals)))/Sum(Budget) ,
if(ValueList ('Actuals Up To Budget','Actuals Below
  Budget','Actuals Above Budget')='Actuals Below Budget' ,
num((RangeMax(Sum(Budget)-
  Sum(Actuals),0))/Sum(Budget),'$#,##0.00;-$#,##0.00') ,
(RangeMax(Sum(Actuals)-Sum(Budget),0))/Sum(Budget) ) )
```

8. Once we define the **Performance** measure, we will notice that just below the Expression box for the measure, we get a dropdown for number formatting. Under this dropdown, change the number format to **Number**. Next, we define the exact format of the number. To do this, switch off **Custom Formatting** and then under the dropdown below that select **Formatting** representation as **12%**.

9. Under **Appearance,** click on **General** and add the `Product Performance` title.

10. Under **Sorting**, set the sort-order for **Performance Type** as `alphabetically` and `Descending`.

11. Under **Appearance,** click on **Presentation** and pick the style for the chart as **stacked** and **Horizontal**.

12. Under **Colors** and **Legend**, switch off **Auto Colors** to activate custom colors.

13. Along with the custom colors, a dropdown to define the colors is also activated. This is situated right below the colors switch. Under this dropdown select **By expression**.

14. Add the following expression under the color expression:

```
if(ValueList('Actuals Up To Budget','Actuals Below
  Budget','Actuals Above Budget')='Actuals Up To
  Budget',rgb(234,234,234),
if(ValueList('Actuals Up To Budget','Actuals Below
  Budget','Actuals Above     Budget')='Actuals Below
  Budget',rgb(255,0,0),rgb(0,255,0) )
    )
```

15. Make sure that **The expression is a color code** is checked.

16. The resulting chart will look like the following screenshot:

## How it works...

The chart in this recipe shows the user the relative performance of each product. The colored segments highlight the extent by which a product has exceeded or failed to reach the budgeted value. The Green segment indicates that the product has fared well while the Red segment indicates that the product is below the budgeted figure.

The preceding example makes use of the `ValueList` function in both dimension and measure. For dimension, this results in three string values, namely "Actuals Up To Budget", "Actuals Below Budget", and "Actuals Above Budget" as row labels, which are further referenced in the measure.

The measure takes the values from the dimension and references them in a nested `If` statement as an input to three aggregated calculations.

We use the `ValueList` function in this recipe as Qlik Sense doesn't allow you to have custom colors for each measure, which we needed in order to do the highlighting.

## There's more...

The same information can be conveyed using a CapVentis Redmond Pie Gauge, the credit for which goes to Stephen Redmond, former CTO of Capventis. The Redmond Pie Gauge chart can be accessed on Qlik Branch at `http://branch.qlik.com/projects/showthread.php?159-CapVentis-Redmond-Pie-Gauge-for-Qlik-Sense&highlight=redmond+pie+gauge.`

## See also

 ▸  *Use the Colormix function*

# Associating persistent colors to field values

The best practices say that a designer should avoid using bar charts with multi-colored bars or having too many colors in any of your chart objects. But at times, we need to cater to the demands of the organization and take an uncalled for approach to designing. The following recipe explains how to associate distinct field values to different colors in the Qlik Sense script.

## Getting ready

This recipe serves to be a good example to demonstrate the use of `Pick` function in the script. Use the following steps to get started:

1.  Create a new Qlik Sense application and name it `Persistent Colors`.

2.  Open the data load editor.

3.  Load the following script that contains information about the `Actuals` and `Budget` of four products. The script is available for download on the Packt Publishing website:

```
ProductsTemp:
LOAD * INLINE [
Product, Actuals, Budget
Footwear, 100000, 120000
Tyres, 180000, 150000
Mountain Bikes, 250000, 195000
Road Bikes, 200000, 225000
];

Products:
LOAD *,
```

```
pick(match("Product", 'Footwear', 'Tyres', 'Mountain
  Bikes', 'Road Bikes'), RGB(236,129,0),RGB(250,185,0),
  RGB(70,137,164), RGB(141,25,8)) as "Product color"

RESIDENT ProductsTemp;

Drop table ProductsTemp;
```

## How to do it...

1. Open the **App overview** and create a new sheet.

2. Create a bar chart on the sheet.

3. Use **Product** as dimension.

4. Use **Sum** (Actuals) as measure. Label it as `Actuals`.

5. Under **Colors** and **Legend**, switch off **Auto Colors** to activate custom colors.

6. Along with the custom colors, a dropdown to define the colors is also activated. This is situated right below the colors switch. Under this dropdown, select **By expression**.

7. Add the following expression under the color expression:

   `=[Product color]`

8. Make sure that **The expression is a color code** is checked.

9. The result would be as follows:

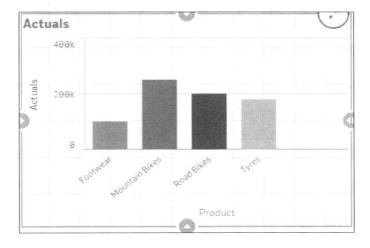

## How it works...

The `Pick` function used in the script links values in the `Product` field to distinct RGB values. Each product is displayed in a different color bar when the `Product color` field is used in the color expression of the chart.

## There's more...

Persistent colors can also be obtained through the chart properties when we select the colors by dimension. However, using this approach we can't have custom colors but have to depend on the color scheme in Qlik Sense.

## See also

> ▶ Use of `ColorMix1` function to establish a color gradient in charts

# Using the ColorMix1 function

Heat maps are a common requirement in most of the BI implementations. A `Colormix1` function helps to create a gradient between two colors. Look at the following recipe to understand the use of this function.

## Getting ready

We will make use of a simple Inline load for this recipe. Perform the following steps to get started:

1. Create a new Qlik Sense application. Name it `HeatMaps_Colormix1`.

2. Open the data load editor.

3. Load the following script that gives you information about `Actuals` and `Budget` for products:

```
Products:
LOAD * INLINE [
Product, Actuals, Budget
Footwear, 100000, 120000
Tyres, 180000, 150000
Mountain Bikes, 250000, 195000
Road Bikes, 200000, 225000
Chains, 80000, 90000
Helmets, 240000,160001
Gloves, 56000,125000
```

```
Pedals, 45000,100000
Rucksacks, 300000,450000
];
```

## How to do it...

1.  Open the **App overview** and create a new sheet.

2.  Create a bar chart on the sheet

3.  Use **Product** as dimension.

4.  Use **Sum** (Actuals) as measure and label it as `Actuals`.

5.  Switch off **Auto Colors** to activate custom colors under **Colors** and **Legend**,.

6.  Along with the custom colors, a dropdown to define the colors is also activated. This is situated right below the colors switch. Under this dropdown, select **By expression**.

7.  Add the following expression under the color expression:

    ```
    colormix1(sum(Actuals) / $(=max(aggr(sum(Actuals),
        Product))), white(), RGB(0, 70, 140))
    ```

8.  Under **Sorting**, promote **Sales** above **Product** in the order of priority. This can be done by holding the ≡ button and dragging it to **Sales** above **Priority**.

9.  Set the **Sort** order for **Sales** as **Sort numerically** and **Descending**.

10. Make sure **The expression is a color code** is checked.

11. The result will be as follows:

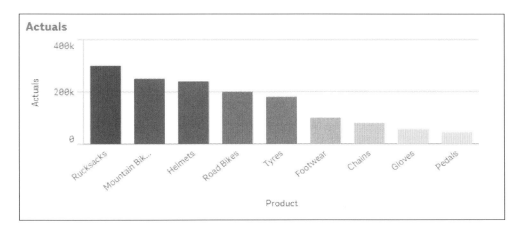

## How it works...

The `colormix1` function creates a gradient between two colors using a number that varies from 0 to 1.

We know that the bar for the product with the highest value of `Actuals` will be the most intense. So to achieve a value between 0 and 1, we calculate the relative shares of each actual value against the highest actual value from the entire product range. That is "Actuals for each product"/"The highest Actuals value from the entire product range".

In our expression, the `Colormix1` function helps to establish a gradient from white to RGB (0, 70, 140).

## There's more...

A sequential color gradient across the chart can be obtained through the chart properties if we select the color by measure. However, we can't have custom colors if we use this approach and we will have to depend on the color scheme in Qlik Sense.

## See also

Similar to `Colormix1`, we can also use the `Colormix2` function, which gives us an option to have an intermediate color between the lower and upper limit color.

# Composition

Composition can be defined as looking at a particular measure compared to the whole.

For example, In a "Sales by Region" chart, the sales for each singular region would be a discrete value while the total sales across all countries would be the "Whole".

Total sales can be divided into "Relative shares" for each region. Having information on "Relative Sales Percentages" as compared to the total sales has a greater impact rather than viewing just the plain sales figures. Eureka moments are much more likely when people use a tool to answer their own questions, which is a core belief behind the design of Qlik Sense.

As with everything else, data composition can be visualized in multiple ways. Understanding what you are trying to achieve will eventually dictate the best choice of visualization.

For example, depending on what matters, each of the following points will favor a different form of visualization:

- Relative differences
- Relative and absolute differences
- Share of the total

- ▸ Accumulation to the total (or subtraction)
- ▸ Breaking down components of components

As such, each example in the next four recipes will be supported by a goal, questions, and an analysis description, which is as follows:

- ▸ **Goal**: As a business analyst, I want to report on the best regions to focus our marketing strategy on
- ▸ **Question**: I want to see how our total revenue is shared this year across the various regions
- ▸ **Analysis**: How the total revenue is divided per region and if it is performing positively

## Getting ready

Downloading the source files:

> **Downloading the example code**
>
> You can download the example source files from your account at http://www.packtpub.com, for all Packt books that you have purchased. If you have purchased the book elsewhere, you can visit http://www.packtpub.com/support and register to have the files e-mailed directly to you.

Use the following steps to get started:

- ▸ Download `Chapter 2 - Sales.qvf` application from the Packt Publishing website
- ▸ Save the application at the following location: `C:\Users\<user>\Documents\Qlik\Sense\Apps`
- ▸ Open the application though the Qlik Sense hub

## How to do it...

1. Click the button in the top right-hand corner in the application overview and click the **Create New Sheet** button. Name this sheet as `Composition`.
2. Go to the charts asset pane  and double click the line chart button 〰.
3. Add the following measure (m) and dimensions (d) in the same order as follows:
   - (m)  `Sum(Sales)`
   - (d)  `Month`
   - (d)  `Region`

4. Select **Area** from the properties pane under the **Appearance | Presentation** menu.

5. Finally, tick the **Stacked area** box. The following screenshot is an example of the final visualization:

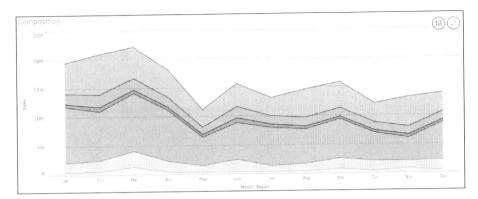

## How it works...

Enabling the right property settings can turn a line chart into a stacked area chart. This clearly shows the differences when we analyze the relative and absolute composition of many time periods, as shown in the preceding example. If you had less time, say the last 3 years, then you would use the same approach, however; you will change the chart type to **Bar** instead of **Line** as the magnitude of change is more important than the change trend.

## There's more...

When looking at the composition in terms of accumulation or subtraction from the TOTAL, a good option for representation is the waterfall chart. If the only important differences are the relative differences are, then write your calculation as a percentage of Total.

To achieve this, follow the following steps:

1. Replace the `Sales` expression from the preceding recipe with the following:

   ```
   Sum(Sales) / sum( TOTAL <Month> Sales).
   ```

2. Once we define the preceding measure, we will notice that just below the expression box for the measure, we get a dropdown for number formatting. Under this dropdown, change the number format to **Number**. Next we define the exact format of the number. To do this, switch off custom formatting and then under the dropdown below that select **Formatting** representation as **12%**. This will produce the following 100 percent stacked area chart:

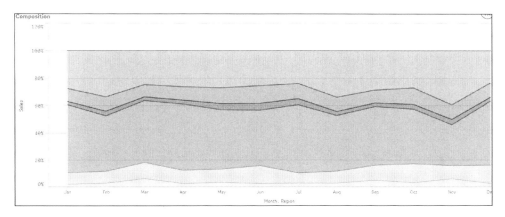

# Relationships

Seeing relationships in data is something that is very difficult to achieve when we view data numerically. The following visualizations are the key to uncovering correlations, outliers and clusters in the data:

- **Goal**: Increase product subscriptions

- **Question**: Are there any differences in the relationship between the revenue and the Sales Quantity by product sub-group?

- **Analysis**: Here we will use a scatter graph to plot product sales that are grouped by product sub-group

## Getting ready

We will make use of the same `Chapter 2 - Sales.qvf` application used in the "Composition" recipe.

## How to do it...

1. In the application overview click on the button in the top right-hand corner in order to create a new sheet and then click on the **Create New Sheet** button. Name this sheet `Relationships`.

2. Once inside the newly created sheet, go to the charts asset pane [ııl] and double-click on the scatter chart button :•.

3. Add the following measures (m) and dimensions (d) in exactly the same order as shown:

```
(m)  Sum(Sales)
(m)  Sum([Sales Qty])
(m)   Sum(Margin)
(d)   Product Sub Group
```

4. In the properties pane, under **Apperance** | **Colors** and **legend**, switch-off the **Auto colors**. Then select **By expression** from the drop-down menu.

5. Finally, add the following expression into the area provided below the dropdown menu:

```
IF([Product
   Line]='Drink',ARGB(100,255,0,0),ARGB(100,0,0,255))
```

6. The final visualization should resemble the following screenshot:

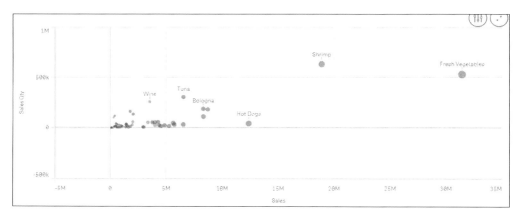

## How it works...

Since the nature of product sub-group dimension is hierarchical, we can actually show two relationships. The first is between the different measures whereas the second looks at the relationships between different product sub-group categories by coloring them seperately.

# Comparison

The bar graph is one of the most common data visualizations. This is because it is simply the best way of comparing the difference in value across a single item.

- ▸ **Goal**: Increase product subscriptions
- ▸ **Question**: Why does a sub set of similar products not respond as positively as others in the same market?
- ▸ **Analysis**: Combo chart

## Getting ready

We will make use of the same `Chapter 2 - Sales.qvf` application used in the "Relationships" recipe.

## How to do it...

1. From the application overview click the button in the top right-hand corner and click the **Create New Sheet** button. Name this sheet `Comparison`.

2. Once inside the newly created sheet, go to the charts asset pane **⊞** and double click the **Combo chart** button ⊯ Combo chart.

3. Add **Product Group** as a dimension.

4. Next add **Sum (Sales)** as the first measure. Label it `Sales`.

5. Add **sum ([Sales Qty])** as the second measure. Label it `Sales Qty`.

6. For the `Sales Qty` measure:

   ❑ Change the default display-format for the expression from **Bars** to **Marker**

   ❑ Right below the display format options, there is a dropdown to define the axis.

   ❑ Set the axis to secondary. Just below the axis formats there is a markers style dropdown. Select the style as **Line**.

7. Under **Sorting**, promote **Sales** to the top of the list.

8. The visualization should resemble the following image:

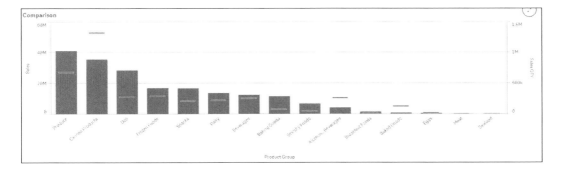

## How it works...

When it comes to comparing the magnitude of change of the values against each other, you really cannot beat a bar chart. When you need to compare multiple dimensions in the same visualization, a common approach is to stack them on top of each other. This option is available in the properties of the bar chart object.

However, this removes the length comparison we are so good at, thus making the view not as effective.

The preceding method of using symbols instead of additional bars still leaves a good focus on the comparitive length to determine the magnitude of change. This is also a more efficient use of space than creating separate visualizations to cover additional analysis.

## See also

> ▸ *Highlighting the performance measure in a bar chart*

# Distribution

Distribution analysis takes a look at how quantitative values are distributed along an axis, from the lowest to the highest. The characteristics emerge while looking at the shape of the data, such as central tendency, shape and outliers:

> ▸ **Goal**: To understand, which demographics should be focused on for our marking approach for a specific product group

> ▸ **Question**: The suitable age-range to target our new marketing campaign towards

> ▸ **Analysis**: Use a histogram to see a useful range from the mean age

## Getting ready

We will make use of the same `Chapter 2 - Sales.qvf` application which we have used in the "Comparison" recipe.

## How to do it...

1. In the application overview, click on the button in the top right-hand corner and click on the **Create New Sheet** button. Name this sheet `Distribution`.

2. Once inside the newly created sheet, go to the charts asset pane and double click on the bar chart button.

3. In the properties pane to the right of your screen, click on **Add** data and select **Dimension**.

4.  Click on the $fx$ button for the input box of dimension and enter the following pre-calculated dimension. Label the dimension as `Age`.

    ```
    =Aggr(Class(Age/19,1),Order)
    ```

5.  Add the following line as the measure and label it `Order Count`.

    ```
    Count(Order)
    ```

6.  In the Properties panel, select **Age** under **Sorting** and check **Sort numerically**. In the dropdown located right below the **Sort numerically** check box, select the order as **Ascending**.

7.  The final distribution chart should look like the following screenshot:

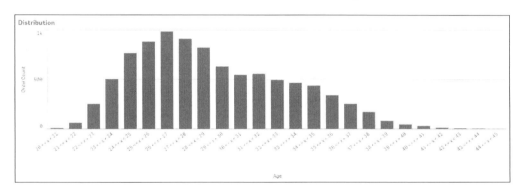

## How it works...

Distribution visualizations help you to analyze one or two variables spread along an axis starting from the lowest to the highest. The shape of the data will tell you about characteristics, such as the central tendency, shape and outliers.

# Structuring visualizations

As discussed in the introduction, when choosing visualization you should start with knowing if you are looking at a comparison, composition, distribution, or relationship.

While this helps in answering a single question effectively, this is often to fulfill the goal that you want to see the information from different angles. Structuring visualizations to easily answer "the next question" keeps consistency in analysis.

While in Qlikview it is common to design a user interface with more interaction than simply filtering the data, Qlik Sense is built with a large focus on the business user and analyst. This recipe involves little practical work and instead it carries the torch for the expert designers in the product team at Qlik. Here is an example of how and why you should make use of a screen and not just an object.

## Getting ready

We will make use of the same `Chapter 2 - Sales.qvf` application used in the "Distribution" recipe.

## How to do it...

The charts that were built in the previous visualization category recipe are available as master visualizations in the `Chapter 2 - Sales.qvf` application. As mentioned during the introduction, the reason behind the structure of the previous four recipes was to think of the business question first. If you can answer someone's question about business with each page (tab), you have a book of gold.

1.  From the application overview, click the button in the top right-hand corner in order to create a new sheet. Name this sheet as `Structuring Visualization`.
2.  Open the master items pane.
3.  Under visualizations drag the **Composition** chart into the top left-hand corner:

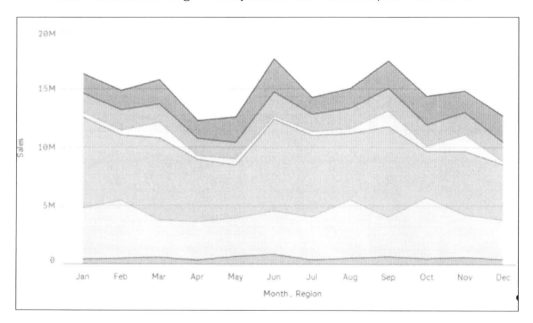

4.   Next, drag the **Relationship** chart into the top right-hand corner:

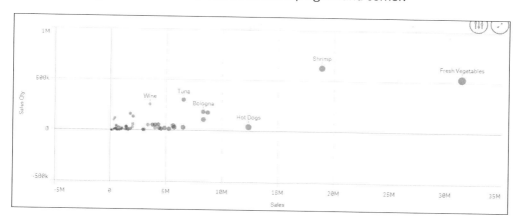

5.   Drag the **Comparison** chart into the bottom left-hand corner:

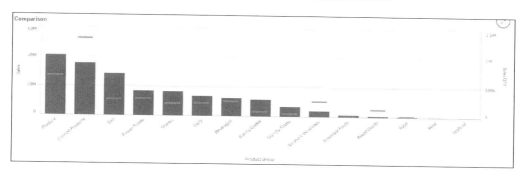

6.   Finally, drag the **Distribution** chart into the bottom right-hand corner:

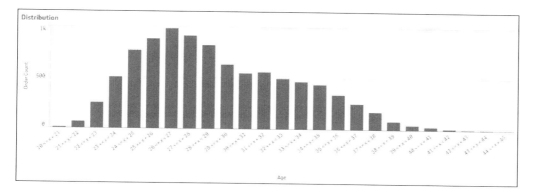

# How it works...

Each of the four preceding recipes has a question to answer for a shared or similar goal. Placing complementary visualizations near each other is good page design. Each chart adds context to the others and helps to build up a clearer analysis picture. The final result should look like the following image. Selecting a point of interest in any of the four charts will show you that the data set from other angles gives you a greater insight with a single-click.

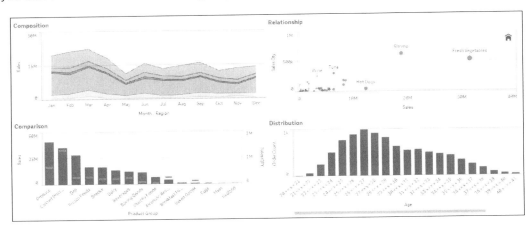

# 3

# Scripting

In this chapter, we will discuss the creation of optimized and well-structured scripts for a Qlik Sense application. We are going to cover the following topics:

- ▸ Structuring the script
- ▸ Efficiently debugging the script
- ▸ Packaging the code in script files
- ▸ How to use subroutines in Qlik Sense®
- ▸ Optimizing the UI calculation speed
- ▸ Optimizing the reload time of the application
- ▸ Using a `For Each` loop to load data from multiple files
- ▸ Using the `Concat` function to store multiple field values in a single cell

## Introduction

What is a script in Qlik Sense? In lay man's language, a script instructs the Qlik Sense engine on how to extract the data from the data source and what to do with it.

It forms an essential component of the ETL process. Hence, it is important to have a well-structured script in order to load the data efficiently. A good understanding of how to optimize an ETL process, leads to a better data model. A good data model is one of the core components along side well written expressions to realize a good user interface performance.

# Structuring the script

The techniques for adding structure to the script is something that comes naturally to experienced developers. This is because they have often learned it the hard way, through other people's work and spent additional time to understand the script that can be made easier with a couple of simple additions. Again, this is something that won't be covered in user guides but it is a very important skill for new developers to have under their belt.

## Getting ready

In this example, we will generate the required data automatically in the script.

## How to do it...

1. Create a new Qlik Sense application and name it `Structuring Scripts`.

2. Create a new section in the data load editor called `Change Log`.

3. Add the following code:

   ```
   /*
   This application demonstrates the importance of adding
      structure to the back end script of your applications

   Change Log:

   [10/06/2015] Philip Hand: Initial build

   */
   ```

4. Create another section called `Calendar` and add the following script:

   ```
   /*============================================================
   Section: Calendar Tab;
   DESCRIPTION: Generates every date between the periods
      vMinDate & vMaxDate;
   DEVELOPERS: Philip Hand, Neeraj Kharpate;
   //==========================================================*/
   TRACE START:~~~~Loading Calendar Tab~~~~;

   Let vMinDate=DATE(Floor(MakeDate(2009,1,1)),'DD/MM/YYYY');
   Let vMaxDate=DATE(Floor(Today()));
   TRACE Calendar date range set to $(vMinDate) & $(vMaxDate);

   Let vDiff=vMaxDate-vMinDate+1;
   ```

```
Calendar:
Load
DateID,
Year(DateID)                      As Year,
Month(DateID)                     As Month,
Date(DateID)                      As Date,
Day(DateID)                       As Day,
Week(DateID)                      As Week;
Load
RecNo()-1+$(vMinDate)             As DateID
AutoGenerate($(vDiff));


TRACE END:~~~~Loading Calendar Tab~~~~;
```

5. Finally, save the data and load the script.

## How it works...

The first tab gives an overview of the application and calls out any key information that a new developer who is seeing the script for the first time will find useful. It also includes a change log to track the changes.

The second tab has a high-level description of the contained code and the developers who have worked on it. Finally, we can make use of the TRACE statements to write information into the execution window. This allows you to see each action being performed during script execution and is a useful tool to debug errors.

# Efficiently debugging the script

It is a good script practice to debug the script in your data load editor before its full execution. This way the developer minimizes the risk of script failures and also saves on valuable time. The process of debugging makes it possible to monitor every script statement and examine the variable values while the script is being executed. The following recipe explains how to debug the Qlik Sense script efficiently.

## Getting ready

Load the following script, which gives information about the Products and Customers in the Qlik Sense data load editor. The sample code is available for download from the Packt Publishing website:

```
Products Temp:
LOAD * INLINE [
```

```
Product, ProductID, Sales
Footwear, F21Lon, 120000
Tyres, T21Man, 150000
Mountain Bikes, MB32Lon, 195000
Road Bikes, RB12Bir, 225000
];

Customers:
LOAD * INLINE [
Customer, ProductID, City
Hero, F21Lon, London
Avon, T21Man, Manchester
Force1, MB32Lon, London
Ferrari, RB12Bir, Birmingham
];
```

## How to do it...

1.  Save the preceding script.

2.  When you save the script Qlik Sense automatically detects syntax issues present in the script, if any. The syntax issues are highlighted in red as shown in the following screenshot. Also make a note of the ⓘ mark beside the section name in the Section panel. This indicates that there is an issue with the script on the tab.

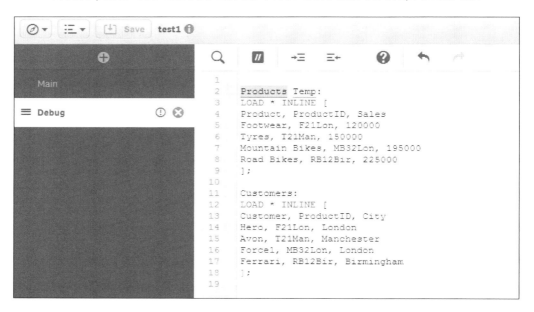

3. Next, click on the Show debug panel  button on the top right corner.

4. A debug panel pops-up from the bottom of the screen with 3 toggles, Output, Variables and Breakpoints.

5. In order to debug the script, load only the limited records, as this will speed up the process of debugging. Keep in mind that when you load limited records from a number of tables in your Qlik Sense script, there may be no records that associate the tables. However, you don't need to worry, as the main concern here is checking the accuracy of the script. Once it is confirmed, the script will run through without errors and you may go ahead and do a full reload.

6. Take a limited load of 10 records by ticking the box for **Limited Load** and entering 10 in the input box. Click on the run ▶ button.

7. On running the debugger, Qlik Sense checks the entire script line by line and looks for any errors. If the script has an error, the execution stops at that point and the issue is highlighted in amber colored box, as shown. The line at which the execution has stopped is highlighted in red:

8. The output window gives us the details of the encountered error. Click on the run button again to complete the script execution. Once the script execution is complete, you will notice that the `Customers` table is loaded fine but the `Products` temp table is not loaded at all. We can verify the same by checking the data model viewer.

9. Check the **Variables** tab. The **ScriptErrorCount** variable gives the count of errors and the **ScriptErrorList** shows the type of error, which in our case is a **Syntax Error**:

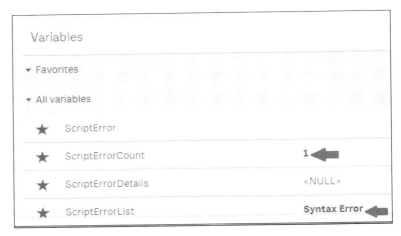

10. At this point, the user can remove the space between the words `Products` and `temp` in the label for the `Products` table to rectify the script error.

11. We can also define breakpoints in our script by clicking on the area besides the line number in the script window. The breakpoints are denoted by ⊖ .

12. The script execution stops at the breakpoint.

13. The breakpoints can be enabled, disabled, and deleted at will by selecting and deselecting them under the **Breakpoints** list or by re-clicking on the ⊖ icon on the number line. The **Breakpoints** are ignored at the blank lines and inside the LOAD statement in the middle of the field list:

14. Alternatively, the user can step through each statement of code in the script by clicking on the Step ▮▶ button.

## How it works...

The Debug panel in Qlik Sense checks through the entire script for errors and makes sure that it is accurate. One major benefit of using a debugger is that the user can load only a few records into the data model for the test. The debugger also allows the user to check the output of the executed script and make sure that it is as desired.

## There's more...

The Debug panel also helps you to identify issues related to variables and fields in the files defined under the $(include) statement. We can also inspect the variables during the script execution. The variables can be accessed by clicking on the **Variables** toggle. One can set any of the variables as favorites by clicking on the ★ next to the variable.

## See also

▸ *Packaging the code in script files*

# Packaging the code in script files

Script files are complete blocks of code that are stored in external files such as `.qvs` or `.txt` and they can be included in your application with a single reference. They are conceptually similar to the subroutines that are covered in another recipe in this chapter. However, there is a subtle difference in the usage. **QVS** simply stands for **QlikView Script File**.

Everything from data sources, expressions, and visualizations can be governed centrally and the script files can be leveraged in a similar way to help build standards in backend data preparation across multiple applications.

## Getting ready

Open a new QlikSense application and create a data connection into a folder where you want to store your script files. As shown in the following example

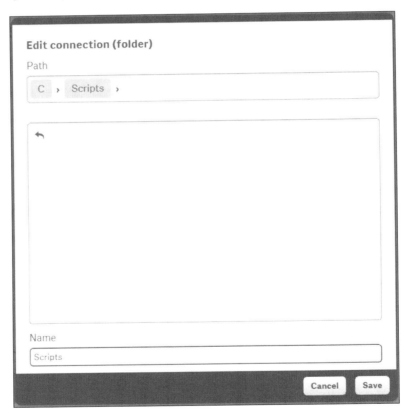

# How to do it...

1. Open a Notepad document.

2. Copy the following subroutine script (a simplified version of the calendar code from the previous recipe) into the Notepad document:

```
SUB Calendar(vMinDate,vMaxDate)

Let vDiff=vMaxDate-vMinDate+1;
Calendar:
Load
DateID,
Year(DateID)                As Year,
Month(DateID)               As Month,
Date(DateID)                As Date,
Day(DateID)                 As Day,
Week(DateID)                As Week;
Load
RecNo()-1+$(vMinDate) As DateID
AutoGenerate($(vDiff));

END SUB
```

3. Save the Notepad file as `Calendar.qvs` into the folder for which you created the data connection. Remember to change the **Save as type** to **All Files**, as shown:

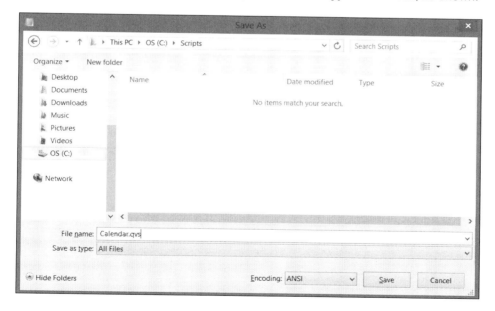

4. Add the following line of code to your application:

```
$(Include=[lib://Scripts/calendar.qvs]);
```

5. You can now call the same subroutine without seeing the code, as in the previous example. In order to generate a calendar, use the following CALL statement in the script:

```
CALL Calendar(01/01/2010,Floor(Today())) ;
```

## How it works...

We have replaced a page of code with just one line using a script file. If you have a code that can be packaged and reused across applications, it makes sense to store this code into a script file for others to use. Doing this reduces the complexity and keeps the focus of new developers on the backend code and on the matter that is relevant to that application.

It's worth pointing out that you could copy the code in the preceding point directly into the script editor and it will still get created and be ready for use. We save this code as a QVS file so that we can load the code using the $(Include...) statement. Loading the script from external files using the $(Include...) statement is a good method of reusing blocks of script across applications or using them for source control.

## See also

▶ *How to use sub routines in Qlik Sense®*

# How to use sub routines in Qlik Sense®

At times, it is mandatory to use the same set of code at different places in the script. To achieve this, developers will sometimes use a copy and paste approach. However, this makes it difficult to maintain and read the script. It is always advised to create subroutines and then simply call them as and when needed.

In the following recipe, we use subroutines to create QVDs and store them in a specific folder. We also generate fields using various functions within the subroutines, which also helps in auditing the QVD files.

## Getting ready

1. This recipe makes use of certain functions such as QVDTablename, QVDNoOfFields and QVDNoOfRecords, which don't work in normal script mode in Qlik Sense. Hence, we need to activate the legacy mode by following the steps given in the recipe titled *How to activate Legacy mode in Qlik sense* in *Chapter 1, Getting Started with the Data*.

2. Once the legacy mode is activated, open Qlik Sense desktop and create a new application called `Subroutines in Qlik Sense`.

3. Create a folder called `QVD` at a desired location on the hard drive. For the sake of this recipe, we are creating the `QVD` folder at the following location:

   ```
   C:\Qliksense cookbook\Chapters\3\QVD
   ```

4. This folder will store the QVDs generated in the subroutines.

## How to do it...

1. Open the data load editor.

2. Create a new data connection called as `QVDFolder`. This data connection should create a `folder` connection to the `QVD` folder created in step 1.

3. In the data load editor, create a new section `Variable Setting`, and add the following code to it:

   ```
   LET vFileName = subfield(DocumentName(),'.',1);

   SET vTable1 =1; //Product

   SET vTable2 =1; //Customer

   LET vQVD='C:\Qliksense cookbook\Chapters\3';
   ```

4. Create a new Section `Data`, and add the following code to it:

   ```
   SUB Create_T_Product

     $(vTable):
     LOAD * INLINE [
     Product, ProductID, Sales
     Footwear, F21Lon, 120000
     Tyres, T21Man, 150000
     Mountain Bikes, MB32Lon, 195000
     Road Bikes, RB12Bir, 225000
   ];
   END SUB

   SUB Create_T_Customer

     $(vTable):
     LOAD * INLINE [
     Customer, ProductID, City
     Hero, F21Lon, London
   ```

```
      Avon, T21Man, Manchester
      Force1, MB32Lon, London
      Ferrari, RB12Bir, Birmingham
   ];
   END SUB
```

5.  Create a new section called `Store_Drop` and add the following code to it:

```
SUB Create_QVD_Standard(vTable,vSub)

   LET vQVDStartTime = num(now());
   CALL $(vSub)

   STORE '$(vTable)' INTO $(vQVD)\QVD\$(vTable).qvd(qvd);

   DROP TABLE $(vTable);

   LET vFieldType = 'QVD_Standard';

   LET vQVDEndTime = num(now());

   LET vQVDTimeTaken = $(vQVDEndTime) - $(vQVDStartTime);

   LET vTableFullPath = DocumentPath();


   TablesLoaded:
   LOAD
   QVDTableName('$(vQVD)\QVD\$(vTable).qvd') AS [STDQVD
   Name],
   Timestamp($(vQVDStartTime),'DD MMM YY hh:mm') AS [STDQVD
   Start Time],
   Timestamp($(vQVDEndTime),'DD MMM YY hh:mm') AS [STDQVD
   End Time],
   Interval($(vQVDTimeTaken),'hh mm ss') AS [STDQVD Time
   Taken (hh mm ss)],
   QVDNoOfFields('$(vQVD)\QVD\$(vTable).qvd') AS [STDQVD No
   of Fields],
   QVDNoOfRecords('$(vQVD)\QVD\$(vTable).qvd')AS [STDQVD No
   of Records]
   AUTOGENERATE (1);

   END SUB
```

6. Create a new section called `Create qvd` and add the following code to it:

```
LET vRunStart = timestamp(now(),'DD MMM YYYY hh:mm:ss');

If $(vTable1) = 1 Then
CALL Create_QVD_Standard('T_Product','Create_T_Product')
ENDIF;

If $(vTable2) = 1 Then
CALL Create_QVD_Standard('T_Customer','Create_T_Customer')
ENDIF;

LET vRunFinish = timestamp(now(),'DD MMM YYYY hh:mm:ss');

LET vRunTime = Interval(num(timestamp#('$(vRunFinish)','DD
  MMM YY hh:mm:ss'))
-num(timestamp#('$(vRunStart)','DD MMM YY
  hh:mm:ss')),'hh:mm:ss');
```

7. Save and reload the document.

8. On the front end, click on edit at the top right hand corner and create a new `Table` object by dragging it across the sheet from the left hand side panel.

9. Add all the available dimensions in the table to get the following output:

**QVD Audit**

| STDQVD Name | STDQVD No.of Fields | STDQVD No.of Records | STDQVD Start Time | STDQVD End Time | STDQVD Time Taken (hh mm ss) |
|---|---|---|---|---|---|
| T_Customer | 3 | 4 | 09 Jun 15 10:53 | 09 Jun 15 10:53 | 00 00 00 |
| T_Product | 3 | 4 | 09 Jun 15 10:53 | 09 Jun 15 10:53 | 00 00 00 |

## How it works...

The first two subroutines named SUB `Create_T_Product` and SUB `Create_T_Customer` create the tables called `Product` and `Customer` and then store the data in these tables.

The third subroutine SUB `Create_QVD_Standard(vTable,vSub)` passes the values of the respective table names and the subroutines. Within this sub routine we also create a number of fields using the load script functions, which are used for our QVD audit purposes.

Further, the `CALL` statements call the subroutines and create QVDs to store them in specified folders.

Along with creating and storing the QVDs, we also get valuable information, such as the number of fields in each QVD, the time it takes to create the QVDs, and so on. It is especially helpful while loading a large dataset.

## There's more...

The subroutines can be stored in an external file and further used in the script using an include statement.

## See also

▶ *Packaging the code in script files*

# Optimizing the UI calculation speed

The following recipe discusses the creation of Flags in the script and the use of these flags in the Chart expressions to optimize the calculation speeds.

A flag can be described as a binary status indicator that is used to indicate certain states of data. For example, creating a new field in the table called `MonthToDate Flag`. This field can be used to flag records with the number 1 if the record was created in the last month, else we mark the record with a 0.

Using this approach, we can now count the number of records in the table that were created in the last month using the expression `SUM([Month To Date Flag])`.

A flag is often used to code complex decision logic into the load script so that the binary "yes" or "no" decisions can be quickly identified from the calculations.

## Getting ready

For this recipe we will generate a sales data in the script as defined in the following script. Load the following script into the data load editor:

```
Calendar:
Load
    DateID,
    RowNo()                               AS ID,
    Year(DateID)                          As Year,
    Year(DateID)&''&NUM(Month(DateID),'00')  AS YearMonth,
    Month(DateID)                         As Month,
    Date(DateID)                          As Date,
    Day(DateID)                           As Day,
    Week(DateID)                          As Week,
    Floor(2000 * rand())                  AS Sales;
Load
RecNo()-1+makedate(2014) As DateID
AutoGenerate(730);
```

# How to do it...

1. In the preceding `Load` statement, add the following line of code just below the `DateID` field:

   ```
   if(Year(DateID)=2015,1,0) AS YearFlag_2015,
   ```

2. Reload the script.

3. Create a line chart with `YearMonth` as the dimension.

4. Add the following measure and label it as `Sales`:

   ```
   sum({<YearFlag_2015={1}>}Sales)
   ```

5. Make sure that the sort-order for the months is maintained as `Numeric` and `Ascending` for the field `YearMonth`.

6. The graph should look like the following:

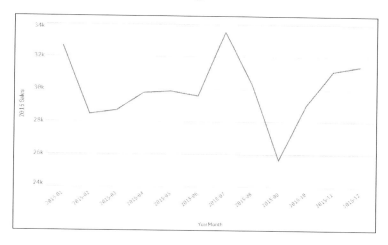

# How it works...

The flag field that we set up simply adds an indicator against the records that fall within the rules we established. Now that we have identified the records from 2015, we can use this flag in the expression to calculate across those records.

The real world difference between using a flag to identify the records in 2015 and just using set analysis to identify the record directly will be almost nothing. The preceding code is a very simplified example of turning business logic into a flag indicator to be used later on. Once you have a grip on the concept and implementation, the same method can be used to add a level of complex and detailed business logic to a binary yes or no flag. Instead of writing the complex `If-then-Else` logic in the chart expressions, it is always advised to move it to the back end script and create flags. The flags are then used in the front end expressions thus making them more efficient.

Adding as much of the business logic to the script as possible makes everything much quicker and simpler to read. This way you don't have to look at each chart before making a change, you can make it in one place only and the change will propagate through the whole application.

# Optimizing the reload time of the application

There are two methods of loading data from QVDs: optimized and non-optimized. The key point here is that the optimized loads can be up to 100 times quicker than the non-optimized loads.

This speed increase is a result of the data passing directly from the disk (QVD) into the memory (RAM) without being unpacked from its compressed QVD format.

As you may have guessed the reason every load is not optimized is because we often want to change the data coming out of the QVD. This requires it to be uncompressed before going into memory; hence, it is significantly slower. Just about any change to the data will cause the load to be non-optimized; however, there are a few things that we can do.

## Getting ready

1. Open a new QlikSense application and go straight to the data load editor.

2. Create a folder library connection to any location where you want to save example data files and call that connection QVDs.

## How to do it...

1. Copy the following code into the data load editor. Please note that if you are using a very low spec machine you can reduce the 20 million number on the third line to something smaller like 1 million:

```
ExampleData:
Load RecNo() AS TransID
Autogenerate 20000000;

Store ExampleData into [lib://QVDs/Data1.qvd] (qvd);
Drop Table ExampleData;

OptimizedLoad:
```

```
LOAD
TransID
FROM [lib://QVDs/Data1.qvd](qvd);


Store OptimizedLoad Into [lib://QVDs/Data2.qvd](qvd);
Drop Table OptimizedLoad;

UnoptimizedLoad:
LOAD
    'Example Text' AS NewField,
    TransID
FROM [lib://QVDs/Data2.qvd](qvd)
Where Not IsNull(TransID);
```

2. Reload the application and make a note of the time it takes to load the records in each table:

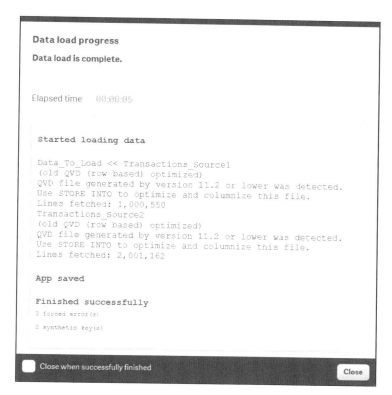

## How it works...

The first 20 million records loaded are simply auto-generated data records that we store in a `Data1.qvd` file to use later on. Now, we have a QVD available to read from, which we can use to demonstrate the difference between an optimized load and an un-optimized load. As a rule of thumb any data transformations on the QVD data in the script will cause the load to be un-optimized.

The second load of 20 million records simply reads the data from the `Data1.qvd` file (created in the preceding step) directly into memory and no further transformations take place. As no transformations take place in the `Load` statement, the load is an optimized load as stated in the Data progress window. We store the data loaded from this step into another QVD file called as `Data2.qvd`.

The third load is from the `Data2.qvd` file, the difference being that this time the script adds a `Where` clause and a new calculated field. Either of these transformations will cause Qlik Sense to use the unoptimized load method. Notice that the **Data progress** window does not specify "optimized load" even though we are loading the data from a QVD file.

You can think of optimized versus un-optimized loads as data being directly loaded into RAM for reading versus the unpacked data that is read line by line. A good exception to a `Where` clause that breaks the optimization rule is the `Exists()` function. Using `Where Exists(<Field>)` at the end of a load is a good method of loading the data that's relevant to what has been loaded previously.

# Using a For Each loop to load data from multiple files

Often in a Qlik Sense application we need to load data from a directory which contains an identical set of data files. For example; sales for each country come in different files for each month. In such a case, we use a wildcard load, in order to fetch the data for our application. The following recipe discusses the data modeling issues encountered when using the wildcard load and how we make use of the `For each` loop structure in the script to overcome this issue.

## Getting ready

For this exercise we will make use of two sample XLSX files, namely, `Apr2015.xlsx` and `May2015.xlsx` that contain mock sales data for six countries. These files can be downloaded from the Packt Publishing website.

## How to do it...

1. Once the source files are downloaded, store them in a folder called ForEachLoadData.

2. Create a folder connection as explained in *Chapter 1*, *Getting Started with the Data* that points to the ForEachLoadData folder. Name the connection as QlikSenseCookBookForEachLoadData.

3. Select any file from the folder and extract its contents in the Qlik Sense application.

4. Next modify the script as the following example, to get the data from all files that reside in the ForEachLoadData folder. Note that we are using a wildcard * in place of the filename in the from statement. The Filebasename() function gets the filename so that we can identify the origin of the data:

```
CountrySales:
  Load
  Filebasename () AS Source,Country, Sales
FROM [lib://QlikSenseCookBookForEachLoadData/*.xlsx]
(ooxml, embedded labels, table is Sheet1);
```

5. Add the preceding load to the script. (the preceding Load is placed directly above the Load statement of the CountrySales table.):

```
LOAD*,
    Left(Source,3) as Month;
```

6. Upon loading, we observe that a synthetic key has been created in the data model.

7. In order to avoid the synthetic key, we will make use of the For each loop along with the wildcard load.

8. Modify the block of code to start with a For Each loop statement and end with a Next, as shown in the following code.

```
For each vFile in FileList
    ('lib://QlikSenseCookBookForEachLoadData/*.xlsx')
    CountrySales:
    LOAD *,Left(Source,3) as Month;

    Load
    Country,
    Sales,
    Filebasename() as Source
    from [$(vFile)]
    (ooxml, embedded labels, table is Sheet1);
Next vFile
```

9. Once the script is in place, save and reload the application again.

10. We observe that all the files from the folder have been reloaded properly and there is no synthetic key in the data model.

## How it works...

The * wildcard character loads all the files from the `ForEachLoadData` folder into the Qlik Sense application. When we use a preceding `load` statement to generate the `Month` field, the load is only applied to the first file loaded from the folder; hence, the `Month` field is created only for the first file. This is the reason why a synthetic key is created between the two tables.

When we use the `For` loop, every file is sequentially loaded from the source folder and then a preceding load is applied; thus, creating a month field in each created table. The two tables are then auto-concatenated, as they contain the same number of fields with the same name. As a result, a synthetic key is avoided and we get a clean data model.

## There's more...

We used iteration or the `For Each` loop in the above recipe outside the `Load` statement. We can also have iterations inside the `Load` statement using the `Where` clause or the `Subfield` function. Iterations are also possible using the `Peek()` function. A useful article from *Henric Cronstrom* on Iterations can be accessed using the following URL:

```
https://community.qlik.com/blogs/qlikviewdesignblog/2013/09/02/loops-
in-the-script
```

# Using the Concat function to store multiple field values in a single cell

The information in orders and invoices is typically stored at the header or line level in the database. However, when we display the sales value for a particular order on the UI, it is sometimes desired that all the products for an order are displayed in a single cell rather than on a separate line. The `Concat` function is helpful in such a case.

## Getting ready

For this recipe we will make use of an inline data load which gives sales information for orders. Load the following order line information in Qlik Sense:

```
Orders:
LOAD * INLINE [
OrderID,Product, ProductID, Sales
```

```
101,Footwear, F21Lon, 120000
101,Tyres, T21Man, 150000
101,Mountain Bikes, MB32Lon, 195000
102,Road Bikes, RB12Bir, 225000
102,Chains, F21Lon, 140000
103,lubricant, T21Man, 56869
103,Mountain Bikes, MB32Lon, 195000
104,Road Bikes, RB12Bir, 65233
];
LEFT JOIN
LOAD OrderID, CONCAT(Product,',') as Products
Resident
Orders
GROUP BY OrderID;
```

## How to do it...

1. Create a Table Chart.
2. Add OrderID as the first dimension.
3. Add Products as the second dimension.
4. Add Sum(Sales) as the measure. Label it Sales.
5. The resultant table should look like the following:

**Orders**

| OrderID | Products | | Sales |
|---|---|---|---|
| Totals | | | 1147102 |
| 101 | Footwear,Mountain Bikes,Tyres | | 465000 |
| 102 | Chains,Road Bikes | | 365000 |
| 103 | Mountain Bikes,lubricant | | 251869 |
| 104 | Road Bikes | | 65233 |

## How it works...

The CONCAT function in the script is used to string together multiple product values in one single string separated by a specified delimiter. The CONCAT function is an aggregation function and would require a Group By clause after the from statement.

## There's more...

The CONCAT function can also be used in the frontend instead of the script. In this case, we will have to create a calculated dimension, as follows:

```
=AGGR(Concat(DISTINCT Product,','),OrderID)
```

Name it as Products. As mentioned earlier, being an aggregation function, CONCAT requires an AGGR that is a substitute of Group By used in the script.

## See also

The *Chapter 5*, *Useful Functions* chapter discusses some cool utilization of functions within Qlik Sense.

# 4
# Managing Apps and User Interface

In this chapter, we will be dealing with the User Interface in Qlik Sense.

- ▸ Publishing a Qlik Sense® application on Qlik Sense® desktop
- ▸ Creating private, approved and community sheets
- ▸ Publishing a Qlik Sense® application on Qlik Sense® cloud
- ▸ Creating geo maps in Qlik Sense®
- ▸ Effectively using the KPI object in Qlik Sense®
- ▸ Creating Tree Maps
- ▸ Creating a Sales versus Target gauge chart in Qlik Sense®
- ▸ Creating dimensionless bar charts in Qlik Sense®
- ▸ Adding Reference Lines to trendline charts
- ▸ Creating text and images
- ▸ Applying limitations to charts
- ▸ Adding thumbnails – a clear environment
- ▸ Navigating many data points in a scatter chart

# Introduction

The information required for analysis and decision making within an organization is communicated via the user interface in Qlik Sense. We discussed the best design practices in *Chapter 2, Visualization*. We will take this discussion a step further and learn to implement a few key objects found in Qlik Sense in our applications, which will help the business convey the desired information to the end user in an effective manner. The chapter starts with important concepts in managing the Qlik Sense applications, such as publishing the apps on the server and on the Qlik Sense cloud. In later parts, the chapter deals with topics such as "Use of Reference Lines" and "Navigating Data Points in Scatter Chart" in a Qlik Sense application.

# Publishing a Qlik Sense® application created in Qlik Sense® desktop

The licensing model of Qlik would not be very useful if everyone used Qlik Sense desktop only for themselves. In a published BI environment, simply creating an application in Qlik Sense Desktop will not suffice. It has to be made available to the end user. The application needs to be published via the Qlik Sense management console.

## Getting ready

Install Qlik Sense Server 2.1.1. The steps to install the Sense Server can be found under the Deploy section in the left panel on the Qlik Sense help website:

```
https://help.qlik.com/sense/2.1/
```

The Qlik Sense Installer file can be obtained from www.qlik.com. You need to login using the customer account credentials to get access to the files under **Support | Customer Downloads**.

## How to do it...

Any Qlik Sense application that is created in Qlik Sense desktop needs to be imported using the Qlik Sense management console prior to its publishing.

1. To do this, open the Qlik Sense QMC through the windows shortcut or use the following URL:

   ```
   https://<Qlik Sense Server Hostname>/QMC
   ```

2. In the QMC, click on **Apps** in the left pane and go to the **Apps** section.
3. Click on the **Import** button in the top right hand corner.

4.  Click on **Choose File** and select the required application to be uploaded and press **Import**. Once imported, select the app and click **Publish** in the action bar.

5.  You will be prompted to specify a stream for the application. Choose a stream from the defined streams in the dropdown menu.

## How it works...

Publishing an application is the first step towards sharing the application with a wider set of end users. Once published the layout of the application cannot be changed. Also, the publishing of the application cannot be undone and you will have to delete the application to remove it from the stream. A better approach to handle such a situation is to duplicate the application without publishing it and make the desired changes to the duplicate application. We can then use the option of **Replace existing app** to replace a published app.

## There's more...

Sheets and bookmarks can be published and categorized as private, approved, or community. This will be discussed in the next recipe.

# Creating private, approved, and community sheets

Sheets are the key components of a Qlik Sense application. They contain all the objects that carry information and provide framework for analysis. There are three types of sheet that can be defined in a Qlik Sense application. These are the private, approved, and community sheets.

▸  Approved sheets are all sheets that are defined by the author of the application. These cannot be changed by the user and are defined as read only.

▸  Private sheets can be viewed only by the author of the application. These are not yet published for access by the end user.

▸  Community sheets are also private sheets but are defined and published by a user other than the author who has been granted access to the application on the hub.

## Getting ready

Sheets can be defined as private, approved or community once the application has been imported to the Qlik Sense Management Console to be published and made available to the end users.

## How to do it...

1. Once the application is published, all the sheets in the application become "Approved" sheets; approved sheets are read only.

2. The "Approved" Sheet cannot be modified unless duplicated as a "Private" sheet. As the name suggests, Private sheets are private to the author. In order to duplicate a sheet, right click on the sheet and select **Duplicate Sheet** option.

3. Once the Sheet is made "Private", modifications can be made to the relevant sheet if required. The sheet can then be published by right clicking and selecting **Publish Sheet**.

4. "Private" sheets can also be created by "Creating a new Sheet" in the published application.

5. Sheets can be created by other users and published to the hub. Sheets published in such a way are categorized as "Community" sheets.

## How it works...

Only the published sheets can be accessed by the end users. Sheets kept as private or approved are not shared until published; hence, they add a layer of security. The concept of community sheets brings in the collaborative feature, wherein the other users can contribute and share objects and reports created by them.

## There's more...

On a similar note, one can create private, approved, and community bookmarks in Qlik Sense. The idea and approach remain similar.

## See also

▸ *Publishing a Qlik Sense® application created in Qlik Sense® desktop*

# Publishing a Qlik Sense® application to Qlik Sense® cloud

Qlik has come up with this wonderful concept of sharing Qlik Sense applications in the cloud. The author can share applications on the cloud with up to five people by sending an e-mail invitation. These applications can be viewed on any mobile device and on any web browser. In a small implementation, Qlik Sense cloud can be particularly helpful as one can share the applications over the web without installing the Sense Server.

## Getting ready

Create a Qlik Sense Cloud account at `https://qlikcloud.com/login`.

## How to do it...

1.  The Qlik Sense Cloud web page appears like the following screenshot:

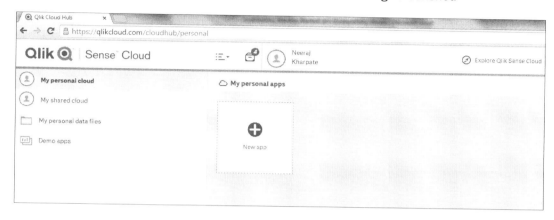

2.  Under **My personal cloud**, Click on the 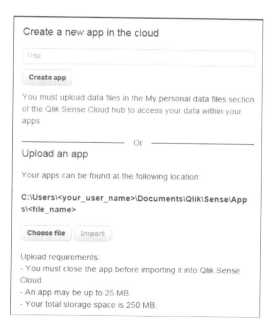 button to import the desired Qlik Sense application to the cloud:

3. Under **Upload an app**, click on the **Choose file** button to select the Qlik Sense application. The Qlik Sense applications are by default stored under:

```
'C:\Users\<\*your own user
    folder*>\Documents\Qlik\Sense\Apps'
```

4. Select the desired application and click on the **Import** button.

5. At this stage, the application can be published to the shared stream by checking the **Publish this app to my shared stream** check box.

6. If the application is not published to the shared stream, it will appear in the **Personal** cloud on successful upload.

7. If the application is published on the shared stream, it will appear in the **My Shared Cloud** on a successful upload.

8. Click on **My Shared Cloud**. Here you will find the recently uploaded Qlik Sense applications.

9. Click on the  Share ⑤  button at the bottom of the window and the following window will pop up:

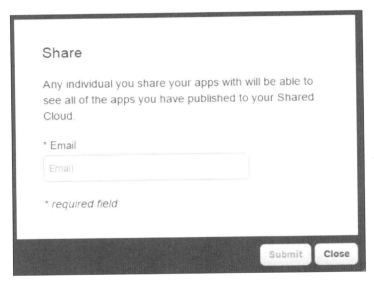

10. Enter the e-mail address of the recipient. The recipient will receive an e-mail with a link to create a Qlik Cloud account.

11. One can open Qlik Cloud while working on the Sense Desktop version by right-clicking on any application and clicking on **Upload to Qlik Cloud**. However, this link does not actually upload the document to the cloud, it only opens the Qlik Sense cloud with the correct dialog:

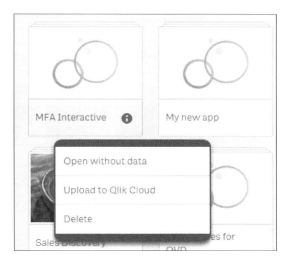

## How it works...

The applications that are published to the cloud can be viewed by any recipient who has been provided with the shared link. Once the recipient registers on Qlik Sense, the author of the application will receive a notification that he has a new follower.

As the information is shared with different users within the organization and outside, it provides the user with a great collaboration feature. Any application in the **My Shared Cloud** area is considered to be shared and can be seen by all followers. It is not possible to share only one application with a particular user. The applications can be unpublished and can be moved to the personal cloud by right clicking and selecting the **Unpublish** option. As of now, there are certain restrictions in using the cloud:

- ▸ The maximum size of the application to be uploaded can be 25 MB.
- ▸ Images and extensions cannot be uploaded to the cloud.
- ▸ While creating new applications directly in the cloud, we can load data only through the files uploaded to the ⬜ My personal data files section or through DataMarket.
- ▸ The followers are not notified if a new application is published to the shared stream.
- ▸ The applications on the cloud can be shared with a maximum of five followers.

## There's more...

Qlik Cloud has the functionality of a personal cloud wherein the author can have his or her own private applications, which are not published to the outside recipients.

Personal data files can be added under the ☐ My personal data files option. Once the files are added under personal data, they can be used to create a new Qlik Sense application in the cloud. The process to create a new Qlik Sense application directly in the cloud is as follows:

1. Select **My Personal cloud** and then click on the ⊘ ▾ button.

2. Add a title to the new application.

3. Click on Create app . This will open the Qlik Sense application in a browser.

4. Open the data load editor to enter the script. If personal data files are uploaded on the cloud, you will notice that a data connection to these files is automatically created within the data load editor.

5. One can also make use of DataMarket to upload data to the application.

6. Add the required data to the script and reload the application.

# Creating geo maps in Qlik Sense®

Geographical information can be plotted in Qlik Sense by making use of the Map object. In order to create geo maps in Qlik Sense, we need to load the location information also called point or area data. The location information can be loaded either from a **Keyhole Markup Language** (**KML**) file, if available, or a database, web service, or from a simple Excel file. Data can also be loaded inline, which is what we are going to do in our following recipe.

## Getting ready

For the purpose of this recipe, we will make use of an inline data load which gives us the location information for different countries in the form of latitudes and longitudes:

1. Create a new Qlik Sense file and name it Geolocations.

2. Add the following Inline table that contains the location information for countries:

```
Country:
Load RowNo() As CountryID, *,GeoMakePoint(Latitude,
    Longitude) As CountryGeoPoint Inline [
    Country, Latitude, Longitude
    Australia, -25.274398,133.775136
    Argentina, -38.416097,-63.616672
    India, 20.593684,78.962880
```

```
      China, 35.861660,104.195397
      Colombia, 4.570868,-74.297333       Great
   Britain,55.378051,-3.435973
      Switzerland ,46.8181887,8.227512
      Netherlands,52.132633,5.291266
      Salvador,13.794185,-88.896530
      Italy,41.871940,12.567380
      Peru,-9.189967,-75.015152
   ];
```

3. Next, add the following `Inline` table that contains the `Sales` information for each country:

```
Sales:
Load * Inline [
      Country, Region, Sales
      Australia,Australia,133775
      Argentina, Latam,6361672
      India, APAC,7896880
      China, APAC,10419397
      Colombia, Latam,742333
      Great Britain,EMEA,3590073
      Switzerland ,EMEA,8227512
      Netherlands,EMEA,521266
      Salvador,Latam,8886530
      Italy,EMEA,12567807
      Peru,Latam,750152
   ];
```

4. Load the data and save the file. Open the **App overview** by clicking on the Navigation dropdown ⊘▾ in the top left corner.

## How to do it...

1. Create a new sheet in the Qlik Sense application.

2. Enter the Edit sheet mode and drag across the Map object from the left-hand side Assets panel on to the sheet. Name it `Sales by Country`.

3. Click on **Add Dimension** and then select **CountryGeoPoint**. Select **Country** to represent the point name:

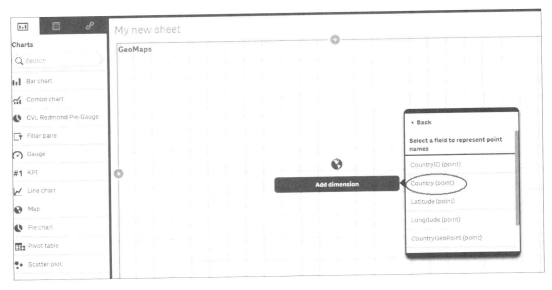

4. In the Properties panel to the right of your screen, add **Sum(Sales)** as your expression under data.

5. The resulting map on the screen will look like the following. The map automatically picks up the Mapbox background in its point layer. The only available image type is slippy map:

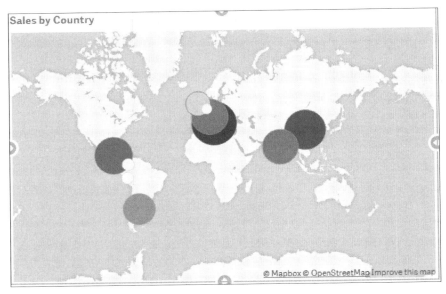

6. Next, we will change the background of the map.

7. To do this, open the Properties panel and click on **Background**. The **Background** windows **Show** property is by default set to **On**. The **URL** and **Attribution** boxes get activated when you switch the **Map service** from **Auto** to **Custom**.

8. Click on the **URLs and attributions** hyperlink at the bottom of the **Background** window:

9. From the available list of slippy map servers, copy a URL and paste it into the **URL** text field.

10. Next, copy the attribution string for the chosen URL and paste the string into the **Attribution** text-field.

11. For the sake of our exercise, we will use the **URL** and **Attribution** string for MapQuest-OSM.

12. Click on 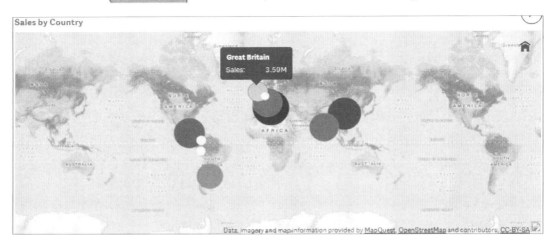 . The final map will look like the following screenshot:

Sales by Country

13. When we hover over any bubble, the tool tip shows the relevant country and sales.

## How it works...

While loading the script for this recipe, we made the use of the GeoMakePoint() function. This function creates and tags a point with its latitude and longitude information. Each country is thus linked to point data, which is plotted on the map. When we use a KML file as a source, Qlik Sense automatically detects the Geopoint field; therefore, there is no need to use a special function to define the same.

While changing the background for the map, we insert the required URL that connects to the tile server that we want to use. For copyright reasons, the attribution string should correspond to the desired URL.

## There's more...

Point data can also be read from Excel files:

1. If the point data is stored in a single column called Location, that is, if each point is specified as an array of x and y coordinates and represented as [x, y]. Here x=longitude and y=latitude then:

   ❑ The geospatial coordinates, namely, the latitudes and longitudes should be tagged with $Geopoint so that the field Location is recognized as a point data field.

- ❏ As an example, consider that the `Location` data is being extracted from a file called `Country.XLS` having three columns `Country`, `Location`, and `Sales`; where `Location` contains the point data. The script in such a case will look like the following:

```
LOAD
  Country,
  Location,
  Sales
FROM 'lib:///Country.xls' (biff, embedded labels, table
is (Sheet1$));

Tag Field Location with $Geopoint;
```

- ❏ Run the script and add the point dimension to the map.

2. If the point data is stored in two columns, that is, one for latitude and the other for longitude then:

- ❏ The `GeoMakePoint()` function should be used to generate point based data

3. Similarly, one can make use of the KML files, which contain point data, area data, or both in order to create maps in Qlik Sense. The following URL explains the process of generating maps in Qlik Sense using the KML files:

- ❏ `https://community.qlik.com/docs/DOC-7354`

# Reference lines in Sales versus Target gauge chart

Recently, while delivering a proof of concept, I was asked by a customer if we could create a "Stephen Few Bullet chart" in Sense. This is not possible out of the box because of the simple reason being that the bullet chart involves overlaying a bar chart on top of a gauge chart and overlaying objects in Sense is not allowed. So, I thought of delivering the same result using just the gauge chart and making use of reference lines.

## Getting ready

Load the following script in the Qlik Sense data load editor, it gives information about the `Sales` and `Target` values for four countries:

```
LOAD * INLINE [
Country, Sales, Target
USA, 10000, 8500
UK, 7000, 9500
```

```
Germany, 5000, 4500
Japan, 6000, 6000
];
```

## How to do it...

1. Drag across a gauge chart object onto the sheet from the Assets panel on the left.

2. Click on **Add measure** and type in the following expression. Label it as `Sales vs Target`:

   `Sum(Target)`

3. Under **Add-Ons**, click on the **Reference lines** and add a reference line expression with the following definition:

   `=Sum (Sales).`

4. Label the reference line expression as `Sales`. Change the color of the reference line to red by clicking on the color dropdown.

5. Under **Appearance**, click on **Presentation** and set the **Max range Limit** as:

   `=Sum(Target)*1.2`

6. Select the representation as **Bar** and orientation as **horizontal**.

7. Check the **Use Segments** box.

8. Next, click on the **Add limit** button and add the following limit:

   - Segment 1:

   ```
   =Sum (Target)*0.30
   Click on the segment area to change the default color to
    Grey.
   ```

9. Again, click on the **Add limit** button to create a second segment with the following limit:

   - Segment 2:

   ```
   =Sum (Target)*0.60
   Click on the segment area to change the default color to
     Red.
   ```

10. Finally, click on the **Add limit** button to create a third-segment with the following limit:

   - Segment 3:

   ```
   =Sum (Target)
    Click on the segment area to change the default color to
      Yellow.
   ```

11. Select the color of the last segment as Green. Check the **Gradient** box for the last segment.

12. Click on ![Done] when finished.

13. The resulting chart will look similar to the following screenshot:

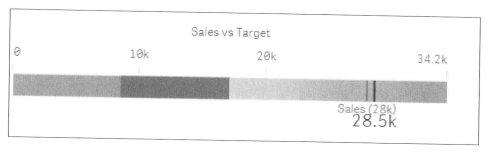

## How it works...

The color segments signify how the sales of a particular country are performing, as compared to the target values. The red reference line indicates the sales value. The color red does not signify anything else and is used only to highlight sales. Hence, you can use any other color of your choice.

The sales can be more than the set target. Hence the **Max range Limit** is set to 1.2 times the target value. Due to this setting, the target value is represented by the black line at the end of the bar. Surely, sales can surpass the targets by more than 20 percent. So, the **Max range figure** can be altered by say to 1.5 times of the target value. One look at the graph and we can easily make out if we are in the red zone or are doing better than expected.

## There's more...

A similar concept is explored in the Capventis Redmond Pie-Gauge Chart designed by Stephen Redmond. The gauge in this object is more of a modified bullet chart. If the sales are more than the target then good performance is shown as a shaded sector to the right of the vertical, while if the performance is below par it is shown as a shaded sector to the left of the vertical, as shown in the following figure:

The Capventis Redmond Pie-Gauge can be downloaded from Qlik Branch at `http://branch.qlik.com/projects/showthread.php?159-CapVentis-Redmond-Pie-Gauge-for-Qlik-Sense`

## See also

▸ *Creating Tree Maps*

# Effectively using the KPI object in Qlik Sense®

A visualization should provide the user with a careful and effective presentation of the data. Numbers have an impact value and they contain a message. Key performance indicators demonstrate the importance of numbers in business and also communicate the health of the business to the audience.

## Getting ready

We will make use of the application from the preceding recipe. The application has the following script loaded, it gives information on the `Sales` and `Target` values for four countries:

```
LOAD * INLINE [
Country, Sales, Target
USA, 10000, 8500
UK, 7000, 9500
Germany, 5000, 4500
Japan, 6000, 6000
];
```

## How to do it...

1. Go to the **App overview** and create a new sheet.

2. Name the sheet as KPI and open it.

3. Go to the Edit mode by clicking on [ ✏ Edit ].

4. Drag across the **#1** KPI object from the Assets panel on to the sheet.

5. Next, add the following measure:

```
(Sum(Sales)-Sum(Target))/Sum(Target)
```

6. Name the label as `Sales vs Target`.

7. Once we add the measure, we can see a host of properties, such as number format, color, and so on, for the measure directly beneath the Expression editor box.

8. For the measure, change the number formatting to **Number** and select the percentage format (**12.3%**) from the available formats under the dropdown.

9. Next, add the limits to define colors. Switch on Conditional colors.

10. Click on **Add limit** and set the limit under function as **0**.

11. Click on the first segment of the color bar and select the color as red with a  symbol .Click on the second segment of the color bar and select the color as green with a ▲ symbol.

12. The KPI object appears as the following:

Sales vs Target

-1.8% ▼

13. Under **Appearance,** click on **General** and Switch on **Show titles** and name the title as `Sales vs Target`.

14. Name the subtitle as:

    `IF(getselectedcount(Country)>0,Country,' ')`

15. Next, go to the **Presentation** dropdown and uncheck **Show Title**.

16. Add the Filter pane object from the Assets panel on the sheet and select the dimension as **Country**. Select different countries to see how your organization is faring with respect to each country:

17. Next, we will link our KPI object to a sheet that shows detailed reports.

18. Create a new sheet called `Reports`.

19. Create a `Table` report on the reports sheet with **Country** as the dimension and the following measures:

    ❏ `Sum(Sales)`: Label it `Sales`.

    ❏ `Sum(Target)`: Label it `Target`.

    ❏ `(Sum(Sales)-Sum(Target))/Sum(Target)`: Label it `Sales vs Target`. For the measure, change the number formatting to number and select the percentage format (**12.3%**) from the available formats under dropdown.

20. Move back to the KPI sheet and enter the Edit mode by clicking on [ 🖉 Edit ]. Select the KPI object. This will activate the Properties panel on the right.

21. Under **Appearance**, go to **Presentation** and switch on **Link to Sheet**. Under **Select a sheet**, select the **Reports** sheet and click on [ 🖉 Done ].

22. When we click on the KPI object on the user interface, it directs us to the reports sheet where you can analyze all the sales and target figures for each country:

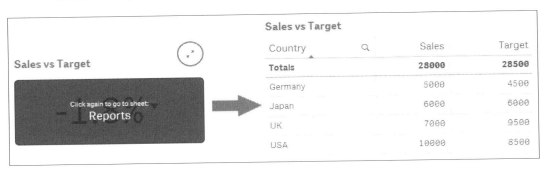

## How it works...

The KPI object is an important visualization object on any dashboard. The color segments we defined in the properties determine if the country is doing better than its set target value or not. If the sales are below the target values then the KPI figure is shown in red or else in green. Linking the KPI to the **Reports** sheets helps the user to dig deep into the data and see the more granular figures.

## There's more...

The KPI object can also be represented using two measures. We can show a comparison between key figures in a single KPI object. For example, the absolute sales and target values can be shown adjacent to each other as separate figures. If the sales are greater than the target then the value is represented in a green color or else in a red color.

This can be achieved by following the steps mentioned in the following steps:

1. Create a new KPI object by following the steps given in the previous recipe. Label the object as `Sales vs Target-1`.

2. Add the following measures:

   ❑ `Sum(Sales)`: Label it `Sales`

   ❑ `Sum(Target)`: Label it `Target`

3. For `Sales` switch on the conditional colors.

4. Click on **Add limit**.

5. Set the limit under function as:

   `=Sum(Target)`

6. Select the first color as red with a ▼ symbol and the second as green with a ▲ symbol.

7. For `Target`, select the font color as **Blue**

8. The resultant object will be similar to the following:

## See also

▸ *Creating text and images*

# Creating Tree Maps

The tree maps (previously called block charts in Qlikview) are a good way to show how different parts combine to form the whole. To add more depth to the visualization, you can easily highlight areas of importance by adding color codes.

## Getting ready

For this recipe, we will make use on inline data load which gives the product sales information. Load the following code into the data load editor:

```
LOAD * INLINE [
    Product Line, Product Group, Product Sub Group, Year, Sales,
    Cost
    Drink, Beverages, Juice, 2015, 12000, 6000
    Drink, Beverages, Juice, 2014, 16000, 7000
    Drink, Beverages, Soda, 2015, 42000, 26000
    Drink, Beverages, Soda, 2014, 68000, 57000
    Drink, Beverages, Water, 2015, 18000, 8000
    Drink, Beverages, Water, 2014, 10000, 6000
    Drink, Dairy, Milk, 2015, 25000, 22000
    Drink, Dairy, Milk, 2014, 22000, 20000
    Food, Dairy, Cheese, 2015, 22000, 8000
    Food, Dairy, Cheese, 2014, 31000, 30000
    Food, Produce, Nuts, 2015, 50000, 30000
    Food, Produce, Nuts, 2014, 46000, 26000
    Food, Produce, Tofu, 2015, 26000, 21000
    Food, Produce, Tofu, 2014, 15000, 7000
    Food, Snacks, Chips, 2015, 31000, 6000
    Food, Snacks, Chips, 2014, 15000, 9000
    Food, Snacks, Dips, 2015, 10000, 6000
    Food, Snacks, Dips, 2014, 6000, 3000
];
```

## How to do it...

1. Drag a Tree Map object onto the content page.

2. Add **Product line** as a dimension.

3. Add **Product Group** as a dimension.

4. Add **Product Sub Group** as a dimension.

5. Add `Sum(Sales)` as a measure and label it `Sales`.

6. From the Properties panel on the right-hand side of the screen under **Appearance | Colors**, toggle the option from **Auto** to **Custom**.

7. In the drop-down window, select **By Expression** and enter the following expression:

   ```
   If(Sum({<Year={2014}>}Sales)>Sum({<Year={2015}>}Sales),
      Red(),Green())
   ```

8. Click on **Done**.

9. The finished result should resemble the following picture:

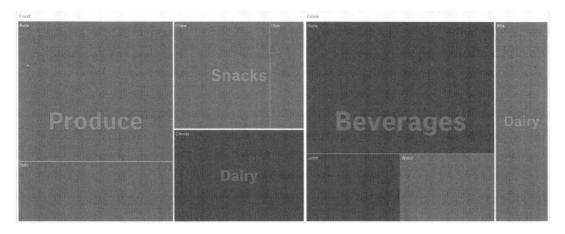

## How it works...

The tree map object groups the data based on the order of the dimensions you added. By adding the color coding expression we can quickly see the products that are doing better this month compared to the previous month.

## There's more...

The red and green indicators used in the preceding image can be useful to spot products that are not performing in-line with similar products. To get more value from these type of indicators, we can change the density of the color to reflect the magnitude of change.

Replace the color expression we used in step 7 of *How to do it...* with the following code:

```
If((Sum({<Year={2015}>}Sales)-
   Sum({<Year={2014}>}Sales))/Sum({<Year={2015}>}Sales)>0,
   ColorMix1((Sum({<Year={2015}>}Sales)-
   Sum({<Year={2014}>}Sales))/Sum({<Year={2015}>}Sales),
   white(),RGB(50,255,50)),
if((Sum({<Year={2015}>}Sales)-
   Sum({<Year={2014}>}Sales))/Sum({<Year={2015}>}Sales)<0,
   ColorMix1(fabs((Sum({<Year={2015}>}Sales)-
   Sum({<Year={2014}>}Sales))/Sum({<Year={2015}>}Sales)),
   white(),RGB(255,50,50))))
```

The chart should now resemble the following image:

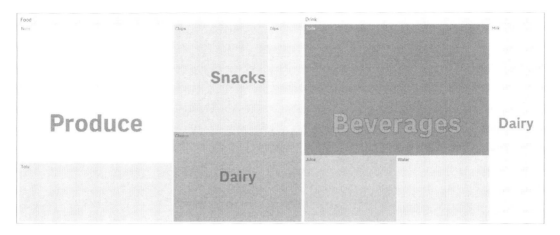

Based on the values returned by the expression, the `ColorMix` function automatically assigns a range of colors. In the preceding example, we have set up two color ranges; the first `If` statement goes from white to green for the positive numbers and the second goes from white to red for the negative numbers. The `ColourMix` function only works with positive numbers, so we use the `Fabs` function to convert the negatives into positives once they are identified by the second `If` statement.

# Creating dimensionless bar charts in Qlik Sense®

A bar chart is usually defined with one or two dimensions and a measure. However, we need to have dimensionless bar charts while designing KPIs on the dashboards and also in certain other scenarios. By default, Qlik Sense will not allow this. However, there is a workaround that is discussed in the following sections.

## Getting ready

We will make use of the same application that we developed for the KPI recipe. The application has got the following script loaded, which gives information on the `Sales` and `Target` values for four countries. In addition, we will add a new column called as `Dummy`.

Make sure to save and load the script once the `Dummy` field is added:

```
LOAD * , 1 as Dummy INLINE [
Country, Sales, Target
USA, 10000, 8500
UK, 7000, 9500
```

```
Germany, 5000, 4500
Japan, 6000, 6000
];
```

We want to display the overall sales for the company and change the color of the bar based on the threshold value.

## How to do it...

1. Go to the **App overview** and create a new sheet.

2. Name the sheet as `Dimensionless Bar Chart` and open it.

3. Go to the Edit mode by clicking on [ ✎ **Edit** ].

4. From the Assets panel, drag across the ▮▮ Bar chart object on the sheet.

5. Go to the **Master Items** 🔗 in the Assets panel and create a dimension with the name `Dummy` as shown:

   `=Valuelist('Dummy')`

6. In the chart under **Dimensions**, use the just created master dimension **Dummy** as the dimension.

7. Add the measure as **Sum(Sales)** and label it as `Sales`.

8. Under **Appearance**, click on **Presentation** and make the chart as **Horizontal** and switch on the **Value Labels**.

9. Under **Appearance**, click on **General** and add `Company Sales` as the **chart Title** under the **General** properties.

10. Under **Appearance**, click on **Colors and legend**. Switch off auto colors and select **By expression** under the drop-down menu.

11. Add the following color code expression:

    `If(Sum(Sales)>Sum(Target),RGB(0,255,0),RGB(255,0,0))`

12. Make sure that **The expression is a color code** is checked.

13. Go to the labels and click on the **Title** option under ▾ Y-axis: Dummy and select **None**.

14. Under ▾ X-axis: Sales , switch off the **Auto** range and select **Min/max** under **custom**. Set the min value to **0** and the max value to **30000**.

15. The final chart looks like the following:

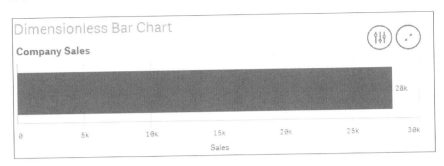

16. Create a Filter pane object with **Country** as the dimension. Now select different countries and view the results.

## How it works...

Qlik Sense doesn't allow dimensionless bar charts. So, we need to create a **Dummy** dimension that has only one single field value. Further when we select **none** under the ▾ Y-axis: Dummy **labels and title** option, it hides this field value from the axis, thus serving the purpose. The color code used for the bars will turn the bar red if the sales for a country are less than or equal to the target values:

## There's more...

We can use the **Dummy** dimension directly from our source data instead of creating a master dimension in the frontend. Another approach is to use a calculated dimension =1 and name it Dummy. All the approaches will yield the same result. To make the chart more informative one can add reference lines for the target.

## See also

▶  *Adding Reference Lines to trendline charts*

# Adding Reference Lines to trendline charts

One cannot overstate the importance of adding context to analysis. Take the example of having the headline number **Average Call Time** displayed on a dashboard. While this might clearly be an important metric for a call center, but on its own it portrays very little. As shown in the *Dimensionless bar chart* recipe in the preceding section, we used reference lines to add the context required to make the number meaningful. Sticking to the example of **Average Call Time**, we may also want to see alongside; a previous point in times position, the national or a competitor's average, the internal target, and so on. This recipe extends the use of reference lines further.

## Getting ready

For this recipe, we will make use on inline data load which gives us the call bounce rates for different periods. Add the following code into the data load editor and reload the Qlik Sense application:

```
WebStats:
LOAD * INLINE [
    Period, BounceRate
    1, 0.26
    2, 0.25
    3, 0.24
    4, 0.24
    5, 0.27
    6, 0.28
    7, 0.21
    8, 0.34
    9, 0.24
    10, 0.25
];
```

## How to do it...

1. Add a line chart object onto the content page.
2. Add **Period** as a dimension.
3. Add **AVG(BounceRate)** as a measure.
4. From the Properties panel | under **Add-ons** click on the **Reference lines** button and then on **Add reference line**

5.  Set the **Label** as `Upper  Threshold` and set the **Reference line** expression to the following:

    `=Avg(BounceRate)+Stdev(Total Aggr( Avg(BounceRate),Period))`

6.  Set the color to red.

7.  Click **Add reference line** again, this time setting the label to `Lower Threshold` and the expression:

    `=Avg(BounceRate)-Stdev(Total Aggr( Avg(BounceRate),Period))`

8.  Set the color to yellow.

9.  Click **Add reference line** for a third time and set the label to `Average` and the expression to:

    `=Avg(BounceRate)`

10. Set the color to green.

11. The final visualization should resemble the following image:

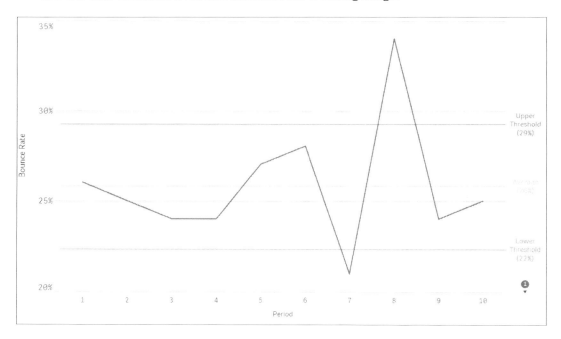

## How it works...

The preceding chart is often referred to as a **Statistical Process Control** (**SPC**) chart. The upper and lower threshold reference lines set a boundary of normal operation. Data points that fall outside of these reference lines differ from the norm and are highlighted as such. The upper and lower limits are simply the average plus or minus the standard deviation. We use the `Aggr` function to "pre-calculate" the average over the period dimension and then apply the `Stdev` function to this number.

Definition: Standard deviation (represented by the symbol sigma, σ) shows how much variation or "dispersion" exists from the average (mean) or expected value. A low standard deviation indicates that the data points tend to be very close to the mean; high standard deviation indicates that the data points are spread out over a large range of values:

```
http://en.wikipedia.org/wiki/Standard_deviation
```

# Creating text and images

Images in Qlik Sense for desktop are stored in the following location by default, `C:\Users\<\*your own user folder*>\Documents\Qlik\Sense\Content\Default\`

Once images have been added to the folder they are automatically made available in Qlik Sense. To add images to your dashboard follow these steps.

## Getting ready

For this recipe, we will make use on inline data load which gives us sales information. Load the following code into your Qlik Sense application:

```
SalesData:
LOAD * INLINE [
    ID, Sales, Quantity, Cost
    1, 15000, 50, 11000
    2, 30000, 100, 25000
];
```

## How to do it...

### Adding Images

1. Place your desired image file into the folder `C:\Users\<\*your own user folder*>\My Documents\Qlik\Sense\Content\Default\`.

2. Add the Text & Image object from the Assets panel to the content area.

3. With the Text & Image object selected, click on 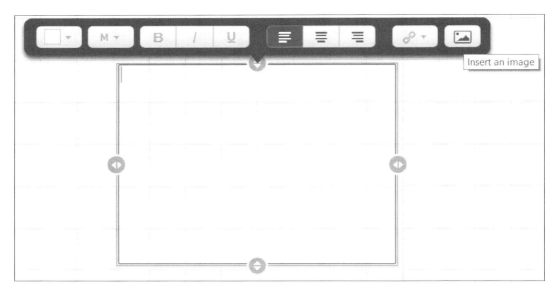 Click to add text and measures to add text and measures.

4. The design bar will appear, click on the **Insert an image** button in the far right, as shown in the following:

5. Select and insert the desired image from the default folder.

6. One can edit the sizing options of the image without clicking on the image button in the design bar as shown in the preceding step. To do this, go to the properties of the Text & Image object and set the same image as a background, using this method now gives you access to size options as shown in the following screenshot:

## Adding Text

1. Add another Text & Image object from the Assets panel to the content area.

2. If you double click on the object in the content page you can immediately start typing the text. You will see some basic formatting options above the object, as seen in the following:

3. Type the following into the text box `Sales =`.

4. Next, from the properties pane under **Data** add the following measure:
   `SUM(Sales) and label it 'Sales'.`

5. From the **Number formatting** drop-down menu select **Number** and from the next drop-down below select the top option with no decimal places (for example 1,000).

6. You can repeat the process using more text objects and different expressions if you like. Multiple measures can be added to the same object or they can be separated out as shown in the following examples:

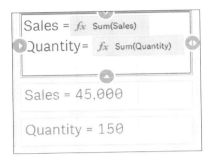

7. An example of text boxes and images is in the following:

## How it works...

Adding text or images to a dashboard can be the key to help users learn more about what they are looking at, not just the company branding.

In the preceding example, we have added a metric into the text box. Normally, we suggest using the KPI object in these instances.

However, text boxes are essential if you wish to add a narrative beyond a single number if all you are trying to do is show one number, using a text box does give the benefit of horizontal labeling. For example the "date of the last reload".

# Applying limitations to charts

While outliers can reveal all kinds of useful intelligence such as issues in data capture or associated process patterns, they can cause problems when you are building data visualizations. The most common issue is to do with scale, as you can see in the following example.

## Getting ready

For this recipe, we will make use on inline data load which gives us the information on the number of call made for each month. Add the following code into the data load editor and reload the Qlik Sense application:

```
Data:
LOAD * INLINE [
    Month, Date, Calls
    Jan, 27/01/15, 25
    Jan, 28/01/15, 27
    Jan, 29/01/15, 25
    Jan, 30/01/15, 600
    Jan, 31/01/15, 22
    Feb, 01/02/15, 20
    Feb, 02/02/15, 19
    Feb, 03/02/15, 21
    Feb, 04/02/15, 1
    Feb, 05/02/15, 600
];
.
```

## How to do it...

1. Add a Bar chart object onto the content page.

2. Add **Month** as a dimension.

3. Add **Avg(Calls)** as a measure. Label it `Average Calls`.

4. Click on **Done**. Notice that the values in both months are just below **150**:

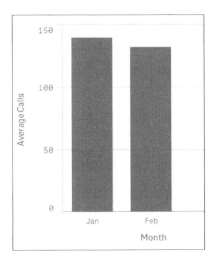

5. Next, go back into the Edit mode and replace the measure with the following code:

```
Avg(If (Calls > Aggr(NODISTINCT Fractile(Calls, 0.1),
   Month) and Calls < Aggr(NODISTINCT Fractile(Calls, 0.9),
   Month),Calls))
```

6. Click on **Done**.

7. The chart should now resemble the following image. It not only has both bars significantly reduced down to below 30, but there is also a much bigger gap between January and February's average call volumes:

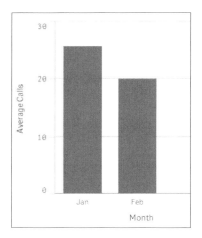

## How it works...

If we look at the source data we loaded at the beginning of the recipe it is clear that there are some outliers present. To exclude these and get a real picture of the normal, average amount of calls, we remove the top and bottom 10 percent of the value. This is done using the `fractile` function. The `fractile` function calculates the cut-off point for 10 and 90 percent based on our data. The `Aggr` function is needed because `fractile` is an aggregation function being nested inside another aggregation.

## There's more...

Another method of handling outliers is not to exclude them from the expression, but hide them from what is visualized. For example, if a data point far exceeds the norm, you can set the axis limit to the second largest value; this focuses the visualization on the points that are closely related. You can do this by going to the object properties:

▸ Under **Appearance**, click on **Y-axis**.

▸ Switch off **Auto Range** and set the **Max value** by using an expression such as the following:

```
=Max(aggr(avg(Calls),Date),2)
```

Here, we simply work out what the second largest number is and set that as the axis limit. This way we can produce an all inclusive line graph by date, albeit one data point will be off the screen.

# Adding thumbnails – a clear environment

It is easy to skip over minor features of a BI platform. Unlike Qlikview, which has a high number of options for chart customizations, Qlik Sense features are more universal. The majority of components will be relevant to you and as such should be given due consideration.

Here, our aim is to simplify the environment by adding thumbnails and metadata descriptions at a high level to the application and the sheets within.

## Getting ready

Open the Qlik Sense Desktop hub and either open up an existing application or create a new one.

## How to do it...

1. Find an image you want to use as the thumbnail for your application. Copy the image into the following folder `C:\Users\*your own user folder*\Documents\Qlik\Sense\Content\Default\`

2. From the **App overview** screen click on the edit  button in the top right corner.

3. Give your application a **Title** and **Description**.

4. Adjacent to the **Title** and **Description** window is the area for the application thumbnail.

5. Click the change thumbnail image .

6. Select the image that you added to the Qlik folder in step one and then click **Insert**.

7. Finally, click the stop editing tick button in the top right hand corner:

8. Depending on the image you have chosen, the color of the background will also change as shown in the preceding image.

9. You can repeat the process for sheets by clicking on the ⓘ button next to each sheet description.

10. You can see a great example of how this should be implemented in the default helpdesk management application that is available with each fresh install of Qlik Sense desktop. Take special note of the sheet descriptions that prompt questions you can answer:

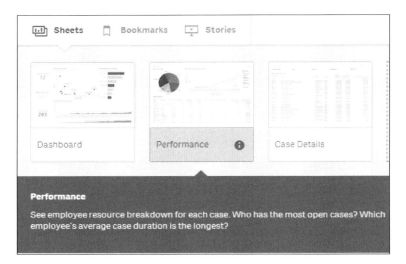

## How it works...

I have seen many unorganized BI environments before and it really has a negative impact on the user experience. When you first go into the Qlik Sense hub what do you prefer to be presented with:

1: Default image and text 2: With Thumbnails and descriptions

The second image looks more pleasing and professional to the eye. User experience is an important factor in adoption of the tool. If the first screen you see looks rushed or is confusing, it will start the user off on a bad foot.

The thumbnails and descriptions also apply to sheets within an application. By default, small thumbnails are displayed as an image showing objects by type and placement. These can be replaced with something clearer and more meaningful to the audience. This is hardly storyboarding, but you should know what each page is trying to achieve. Actually, asking questions about each screen can help you get a feel for the shape of the application and the flow of analysis. Are you asking these questions?

1. Who are the users of this screen?
2. What is the page showing?
3. What questions will the page answer?
4. What actions will that enable?

While not universal, asking questions such as these regularly will help keep your focus on the audience.

# Navigating many data points in a scatter chart

The following recipe showcases an interesting concept in the use of scatter charts in Qlik Sense. This feature is available from version 2.0+ of Qlik Sense.

## Getting ready

Load the following code into your Qlik Sense application:

```
Transactions:
Load
  Round(1000*Rand()*Rand()*Rand()) as Sales,
  Round(10*Rand()*Rand()*Rand()) as Quantity,
  RecNo() as TransID
Autogenerate 1000000
  While rand()<0.5 or IterNo()=1;
```

## How to do it...

1.  Create a new sheet and drag a scatter plot chart object onto the content page.

2.  Add **TransID** as a dimension.

3.  Add **Sum(Sales)** as the first measure. Label it `Sales`.

4.  Add **Sum(Quantity)** as the second measure. Label it `Quantity`.

5.  Click on **Done**.

6.  Title the chart as `Sales vs Quantity`.

7.  You will notice that you cannot select data inside the chart like you can with every other Sense visualization. To navigate the data you have to scroll in and out using the mouse wheel. The object will look like the following image; try scrolling in:

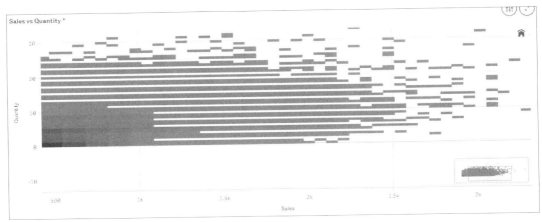

8.  As you zoom further into the chart , the number of data points being displayed reduces at once. You will eventually see the details of each data point displayed in each block. The higher density blocks are also color coded as show in the following:

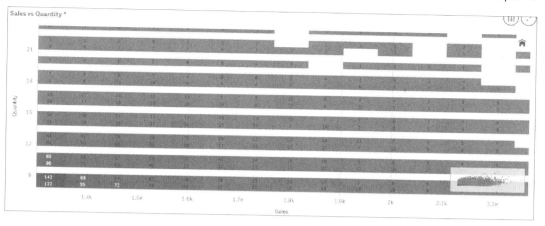

9. Eventually, you can zoom in enough and reduce the number of data points to where they are identifiable individually. At this point the graphic will revert its display to a more standard scatter chart look. Those with enough space around them actually have the value displayed as shown in the following:

# How it works...

This is a very intelligent addition by Qlik to the normal scatter chart display. This chart plots over a million data points effortlessly. Doing this the traditional way is very process intensive. When you want to extract data volumes of this size, you normally tend to look at the pattern and not at the individual numbers. This archives both by displaying the individual points at the point they would make sense and not before.

## There's more...

While the color coding is fixed at the high level you can apply color coding expressions like normal. This only gets applied when you zoom in far enough to see the individual data points.

# 5

# Useful Functions

In this chapter, we will focus on some interesting and useful functions available in Qlik Sense:

- ▸ Using an extended interval match to handle Slowly Changing Dimensions
- ▸ Using the `Previous()` function to identify the latest record for a dimensional value
- ▸ Using the `NetworkDays()` function to calculate the working days in a calendar month
- ▸ Using the `Concat()` function to display a string of field values as a dimension
- ▸ Using the `MinString()` function to calculate the age of the oldest case in a queue
- ▸ Using the `RangeSum()` function to plot cumulative figures in trendline charts
- ▸ Using the `Fractile()` function to generate quartiles
- ▸ Using the `FirstSortedValue()` function to identify the median in a quartile range
- ▸ Using the `Derive` and `Declare` functions to generate `Calendar` fields
- ▸ Setting up a moving annual total figure
- ▸ Using the `For Each` loop to extract files from a folder
- ▸ Using the `Peek()` function to create a currency Exchange Rate Calendar
- ▸ Using the `Peek()` function to create a Trial Balance sheet

## Introduction

In this chapter, we will shift our focus to the functions available in Qlik Sense. In certain situations, the functions can be used in the script or they can be used in frontend expressions to get solutions for complex requirements. All the functions discussed in this chapter will find their way into most of the Qlik Sense implementations.

# Using an extended interval match to handle Slowly Changing Dimensions

Sometimes while developing the Data model for a Business Intelligence application, one comes across dimensional values that tend to change with time. Such dimensions are known as *Slowly Changing Dimensions*. For example, an employee joins a company at a Junior Executive level and stays at the same position for 1 year. After one year, the designation changes to Senior Executive and then changes to Project Manager after 3 years. The position field in this case will be treated as a *Slowly Changing Dimension*.

Such Slowly Changing Dimensions can be represented in Qlik Sense, provided the historical data is stored at the source with a proper "Position Start Date" and "Position End Date".

In order to match the discrete date values to the date intervals, we will make use of the `intervalmatch` function. At the same time, we will match the values of the primary key. This will help us to build an optimized Data model and properly link the transactions to the Slowly Changing Dimensions.

## Getting ready

The following recipe assumes a hypothetical situation wherein an HR department is trying to track the *Employee Journey* within an organization that is tracking the various positions the employee has held within his or her tenure with the company and the related compensation against each position. For this purpose, we will create the following `Inline` tables within Qlik Sense:

- ▸ **2 Dimension Tables**: `Employee` and `Position`
- ▸ **1 Date Intervals table to track changes in position for the employee**: `Employment`
- ▸ **1 Fact table**: `EmpSalary`

The steps to do so are as follows:

1. Create a new Qlik Sense application.
2. Load the following script in Qlik Sense:

```
// ============ Load the Employee table ============
Employee:
LOAD * INLINE [
    EmployeeID,EmployeeName
    11,Susan Sayce
    22,Adam Holliaoak
    33,Rod Marsh
    44,Alex Gerard
    55,Pete Cox
```

```
];
// ============ Load the Position table ============
Position:
LOAD * INLINE [
PositionID,Position
1,HR Analyst
2,HR Director
3,HR Executive
];


// ==== Load the Employee table with the Date Intervals ====
EmployeeInt:
LOAD *,
    Autonumber(EmployeeID & '-' & PositionFrom & '-' & PositionTo)
    as DatePositionKey;
LOAD DATE(Date#( PositionFrom,'DD/MM/YYYY')) as PositionFrom,
DATE(Date#( PositionTo,'DD/MM/YYYY')) as PositionTo, PositionID,
  EmployeeID
 INLINE [
    PositionFrom, PositionTo,PositionID,EmployeeID
    01/09/2009, 31/10/2010,2,11
    01/08/2008, 31/08/2009,1,11
    10/08/2008, 15/03/2010,1,22
    03/03/2008, 08/12/2008,2,33
    15/02/2008, 15/03/2010,3,44
    01/06/2008, 08/12/2008,3,55
];


// ============ Load the Employee Salary table ============
EmployeeSalary:
LOAD EmpID ,DATE(Date#( DateInToPosition,'DD/MM/YYYY')) as
    DateInToPosition, EmployeeSal INLINE [
    EmpID,DateInToPosition,EmployeeSal
    11,01/09/2009,90000
    11,01/08/2008,50000
    22,10/08/2008,45000
    33,03/03/2008,100000
    44,15/02/2008,60000
    55,01/06/2008,55000
];
```

## How to do it...

1. Open the Data model viewer. The Data model is shown in the following figure. We can see that the `EmpSalary` table is not linked to the Data model. If we try to link the table through the `EmpID` field, then the employees who have changed their positions would reflect the same salaries for each position, which is not correct.

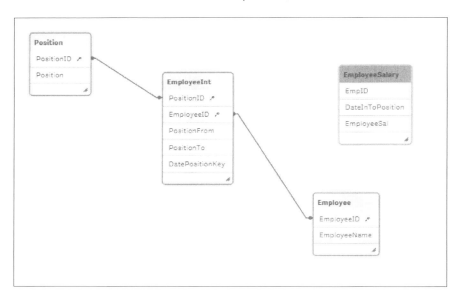

2. Open the **App overview** and create a new sheet. Drag a Table object onto the content area.

3. Add the following dimensions to the table: **EmployeeID**, **EmployeeName**, **Position**, **PositionFrom**, and **PositionTo**.

4. Under **Sorting**, promote **EmployeeName** to the top. Promote **PositionFrom** to the second position and set the sort order as numeric and ascending.

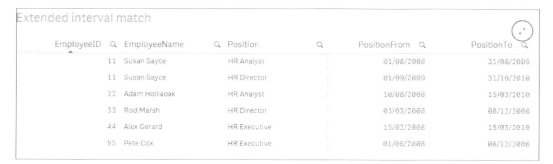

5. In the preceding script, **Susan Sayce** has changed her position from **HR Analyst** to **HR Director**. There is a `DateInToPosition` value associated with each position, which comes from the `EmployeeSalary` table.

6. We will make use of the `IntervalMatch` function, which will match the `DateInToPosition` to the date interval of `PositionFrom` and `PositionTo`.

7. Load the following script on a separate section:

```
// === Link Table using the IntervalMatch prefix ===
LinkTable:
IntervalMatch (DateInToPosition,EmpID)
Load distinct PositionFrom, PositionTo, EmployeeID AS EmpID
  Resident EmployeeInt;

Left Join (EmployeeSalary)
Load
EmpID,
DateInToPosition,
Autonumber(EmpID & '-' & PositionFrom & '-' & PositionTo)
  AS DatePositionKey
Resident LinkTable;

// =========== Cleanup ============
Drop Table LinkTable;
Drop Field EmpID;
```

8. On the final load, the Data model should look like this:

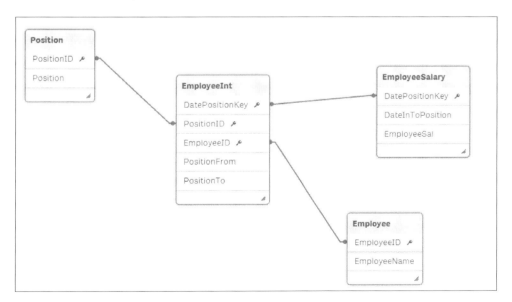

9. Open the **App overview** via the navigation ⊘▾ dropdown on the top-left corner. Go back to the sheet created in step 2.

10. In the Table object, add the following measure and label it `Salary`:

    `Sum(EmployeeSal)`

11. Make sure that the sorting order remains same as mentioned in step 4, that is, to promote `EmployeeName` to the top. Promote `PositionFrom` to the second position and set the sort order as numeric and ascending.

12. The resultant table would look like this:

| Extended interval match | | | | | |
| --- | --- | --- | --- | --- | --- |
| EmployeeID 🔍 | EmployeeName 🔍 | Position 🔍 | PositionFrom 🔍 | PositionTo 🔍 | Salary |
| **Totals** | | | | | **400000** |
| 11 | Susan Sayce | HR Analyst | 01/08/2008 | 31/08/2009 | 50000 |
| 11 | Susan Sayce | HR Director | 01/09/2009 | 31/10/2010 | 90000 |
| 22 | Adam Holliaoak | HR Analyst | 10/08/2008 | 15/03/2010 | 45000 |
| 33 | Rod Marsh | HR Director | 03/03/2008 | 08/12/2008 | 100000 |
| 44 | Alex Gerard | HR Executive | 15/02/2008 | 15/03/2010 | 60000 |
| 55 | Pete Cox | HR Executive | 01/06/2008 | 08/12/2008 | 55000 |

13. Select a particular employee to see all the associated positions, start dates, end dates, and salaries.

## How it works...

The dimension tables are loaded first. A composite key comprising `EmployeeID`, `PositionFrom`, and `PositionTo` is created in the `EmployeeInt` table.

The fact table `EmployeeSalary` is loaded with the `EmployeeID` value represented as `EmpId`.

Under `LinkTable`, an interval is assigned to each combination of `EmpID` and `DateInToPosition` using the `intervalmatch` function.

Finally, a key is created in `LinkTable` with the same combination of `EmployeeID`, `PositionFrom`, and `PositionTo`. The `LinkTable` is joined back to the `EmployeeSalary` table.

The problem of slowly changing dimensions can be solved using the extended `intervalmatch` syntax explained in the preceding steps. The employee, positions, and salaries will all be properly linked.

## There's more...

In the preceding example we have joined `LinkTable` to the `EmployeeSalary` table. However, one should bear in mind that this can only be done if there is a *Many-One* relationship between the **Employee** and **Position**. If this doesn't hold true, that is, if an employee knowingly or unknowingly has more than one position for the same start and end dates in the source data, then the join between the link and the `EmployeeSalary` table will result in an increase in the number of records. In such a situation, the left join should be avoided.

Instead `LinkTable` must simply be linked through the `DatePositionKey` composite key to the `EmployeeInt` table. Another composite key comprising `DateInToPosition` and `EmpID` must be created which should link back to the same key in `EmployeeSalary`.

The resident load for the `Link` table would be as follows:

```
Link:
Load
Autonumber(EmpID & '-' & DateInToPosition)AS DateInToPositionKey,
Autonumber(EmpID & '-' & PositionFrom & '-' & PositionTo)
AS DatePositionKey
Resident LinkTable;
```

The resident load for the `Employee` table would be as follows:

```
EmployeeSalary_1:
Load
*,
Autonumber(EmpID & '-' & DateInToPosition)AS DateInToPositionKey
Resident
EmployeeSalary;
DROP TABLE EmployeeSalary;
```

On loading the script, the resulting Data model would be like this:

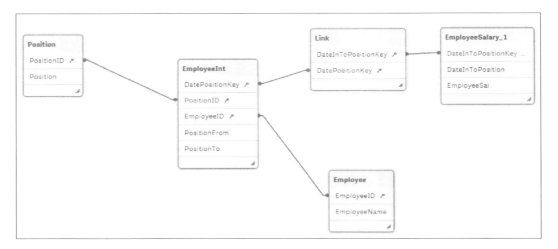

## See also

▶ *Using the Previous() function to identify the latest record read for a dimensional value*

# Using the Previous() function to identify the latest record for a dimensional value

In a line-level table, there are multiple records stored for a single dimensional value. For example, an `Order Line` table will have multiple lines for the same `OrderID`. Business requirements may warrant us to only consider the first or the latest line for each order. This can be done using the `Previous()` function available in Qlik Sense.

## Getting ready

For the sake of continuity, we will make use of the same script and application as in the previous recipe. We will determine the most recent position for any employee during his or her tenure within the organization.

## How to do it...

1. Open the data load editor. Change the name of the `EmployeeInt` table in the script to `EmployeeIntTemp`.

2. Insert the following lines of code after the `EmployeeIntTemp` table. If you are copying and pasting the code in the data load editor, make sure that the single quotes are copied in a proper format:

```
EmployeeInt:
LOAD *,
if([EmployeeID]= previous([EmployeeID]),'No','Yes') AS
  LatestRecordFlag
RESIDENT EmployeeIntTemp
ORDER BY [EmployeeID] ASC, PositionFrom DESC;

DROP TABLE EmployeeIntTemp;
```

3. Save and load the script.

4. Add the field `LatestRecordFlag` in the Table object we created in the previous recipe.

5. Under **Sorting**, make sure that `PositionFrom` is promoted to the top. Switch off the **Auto sorting** feature for `PositionFrom`. No sorting options should be selected as this will then show the `PositionFrom` date in the load order.

6. The table would look like this:

Extended interval match

| EmployeeID | EmployeeName | Position | PositionFrom | PositionTo | Salary | LatestRecordFlag |
|---|---|---|---|---|---|---|
| Totals | | | | | 400000 | |
| 11 | Susan Sayce | HR Director | 01/09/2009 | 31/10/2010 | 90000 | Yes |
| 11 | Susan Sayce | HR Analyst | 01/08/2008 | 31/08/2009 | 50000 | No |
| 22 | Adam Holliaoak | HR Analyst | 10/08/2008 | 15/03/2010 | 45000 | Yes |
| 33 | Rod Marsh | HR Director | 03/03/2008 | 08/12/2008 | 100000 | Yes |
| 44 | Alex Gerard | HR Executive | 15/02/2008 | 15/03/2010 | 60000 | Yes |
| 55 | Pete Cox | HR Executive | 01/06/2008 | 08/12/2008 | 55000 | Yes |

7. Select employee **Susan Sayce**. We can see that there are two positions associated with Susan. If we select the `LatestRecordFlag` value as **Yes**, it will only show the latest position for Susan: **HR Director**.

## How it works...

The `LatestRecordFlag` can be used in calculations to determine the most recent position of any employee. In our script, we create the `LatestRecordFlag` using the `Previous()` function. The `Previous()` function basically parses the `EmployeeID` column. If the current record that is being read has the same `EmployeeID` value as the previous record, then it is flagged as `No` or else `Yes`.

The *ordering* of the fields plays an important role here. Because I wanted to determine the latest position for the employee, the field `PositionFrom` is arranged in descending order.

## There's more...

We can also make use of the `Peek()` function in the preceding script. In our example, both `Peek()` and `Previous()` would yield the same result. However, `Peek()` is more effective when the user is targeting a field which has not previously loaded in the table or if the user wants to target a specific row. The `Previous()` function is more effective when the user wants to compare the current value with the previous value for the field in the input table.

## See also

▸ *Using the Peek() function to create a Trial Balance sheet*

# Using the NetworkDays() function to calculate the working days in a calendar month

One of the KPIs that companies often concentrate on is the average sales in a month. The average sales are calculated by dividing the total sales by the number of working days in a month.

Every month has a different number of working days. While calculating the number of working days for the current month, we only need to consider the days passed in the month and not the total days of the month in order to calculate the actual working days.

In order to arrive at the exact number of working days in a month, we need to exclude all the Fridays and Saturdays as well as the public and bank holidays from our calculations. The `Networkdays()` function helps us to achieve this.

## Getting ready

For this exercise, we first need to prepare a list of all public holidays either in Excel or inline in the Qlik Sense script.

## How to do it...

1. Copy and paste the following part of the script in the data load editor. This is a list of public holidays for 2014 and 2015:

```
HolidayTmp:
LOAD DATE(Date#( Date,'DD/MM/YYYY')) as Date INLINE [
Date
01/01/2015
03/04/2015
06/04/2015
04/05/2015
25/05/2015
31/08/2015
25/12/2015
28/12/2015
01/01/2014
18/04/2014
21/04/2014
05/05/2014
26/05/2014
25/08/2014
25/12/2014
26/12/2014
];
```

2. Next, we will store the list of public holidays in a variable inside the script:

```
ConcatTmp:
LOAD concat(chr(39) & Date & chr(39),',') AS HolidayDates
RESIDENT HolidayTmp;
LET vPublicHolidays = FieldValue('HolidayDates',1);

LET vCurMonth=month(today());
```

3. Copy and paste the following fact table. Insert the last of the `PostingDates` in your table as today's date and put a sales figure against it. This is to demonstrate the use of `today()` in the the `WorkingDays` calculation:

```
SalesTmp:
LOAD DATE(Date#( PostingDate,'DD/MM/YYYY')) as PostingDate,
   Sales INLINE [
PostingDate, Sales
05/08/2014, 5000
04/09/2014,522
```

```
24/10/2014,400
15/11/2014,5000
24/12/2014, 822
29/12/2014, 633
02/01/2015, 1000
02/02/2015, 2000
25/03/2015,2200
25/04/2015,266
09/05/2015, 3000
18/05/2015, 4000
15/06/2015,5000
22/07/2015,456
08/09/2015,4200
26/10/2015,1875
];
```

4. Next, calculate the number of working days:

```
Sales:
LOAD *,
Month(PostingDate) as Month,
MonthName(PostingDate) AS MonthYear,
IF(Year(PostingDate)=Year(TODAY()) AND Month(PostingDate)=MONTH(TO
DAY()),
   NETWORKDAYS(MONTHSTART(today()),(Today()),
   $(vPublicHolidays)), NETWORKDAYS(MONTHSTART(PostingDate),
   MonthEnd(PostingDate),
$(vPublicHolidays))) AS WorkingDays RESIDENT
SalesTmp;
DROP table SalesTmp;
   DROP table HolidayTmp;
```

5. Load the script.

6. On the Qlik Sense sheet, create a table object and name it `Average Monthly Sales`.

7. Add **MonthYear** and **WorkingDays** as dimensions.

8. Add the following measure and label it as `Avg Sales`:

```
Sum(Sales)/WorkingDays
```

9. Set the number formatting for **Avg Sales** to **Money**.

10. Under **Sorting**, make sure that the `MonthYear` field is promoted to the top.

11. Go to **Appearance | Presentation** and switch off **Totals**.

12. The final table object should look like this:

**Average Monthly Sales**

| MonthYear | WorkingDays | Avg Sales |
|---|---|---|
| Aug 2014 | 20 | £250.00 |
| Sep 2014 | 22 | £23.73 |
| Oct 2014 | 23 | £22.22 |
| Nov 2014 | 20 | £250.00 |
| Dec 2014 | 21 | £69.29 |
| Jan 2015 | 21 | £47.62 |
| Feb 2015 | 20 | £100.00 |
| Mar 2015 | 22 | £100.00 |
| Apr 2015 | 20 | £13.30 |
| May 2015 | 19 | £368.42 |
| Jun 2015 | 22 | £227.27 |
| Jul 2015 | 23 | £19.83 |
| Sep 2015 | 22 | £190.91 |
| Oct 2015 | 18 | £104.17 |

## How it works...

The Concat function stores the aggregated string concatenation of all the holiday dates. These holiday dates are stored in a variable vPublicHolidays, which is further used in the Networkdays() function.

The Networkdays() function has three parameters. The first two parameters define the range of dates to consider. If the PostingDate date lies in the current month, the range of dates is defined by the first day of the month and today. From this range, we exclude the non-working days Saturdays, Sundays, and public holidays.

If the posting date is in a month prior to the current month, the first and the last day of said month determine the range of the days for calculating the working days.

## See also

▸    *Using the Concat() function to display a string of field values as a dimension*

# Using the Concat() function to display a string of field values as a dimension

A line-level table is normally the most granular data in a Data model. For example, consider an `Order Line` table. The orders for each customer are stored one row per product line, and we have corresponding costs for each product on each line. When we generate a Table report for such data, we will have a separate line for each product which in itself is not wrong. But recently a customer asked me to initiate an export for the Table report in such a way that all the products for a particular order are contained in a single cell and the sales column should show the aggregated figure for all the products under `OrderID`. To tackle this requirement, I created a calculated dimension using the `Concat` function. The process is explained in the following recipe.

## Getting ready

1. Create a new Qlik Sense application.
2. Add the following `INLINE` table that contains the `Order Line` table details:

```
Orders:
LOAD * INLINE [
     Customer,OrderID,Product,Cost
     1,201,Chain,20
     1,201,Seat,40
     1,201,Mudguard,50
     2,202,Gloves,15
     2,202,Basket,60
     3,203,Helmet,70
     ];
```

3. Load the data and save the file. Open **App overview** by clicking on the Navigation dropdown ⊘▾ in the top-left corner.

## How to do it...

1. Create a new sheet.
2. Drag the Table object from the left-hand side Assets panel on to the sheet. Name it `Sales by Order`.
3. Add **OrderID** and **Customer** as dimensions.
4. Add the following as a third, calculated dimension and label it `Products`:

```
=AGGR(Concat(DISTINCT Product,','),OrderID)
```

5. Add the following expression as the measure. Label it `Total Sales`:

   `Sum(Cost)`

6. Click on **Save** and click on [✎ Done].

7. The resulting table on the screen will look like this:

| Sales by Orders | | | |
|---|---|---|---|
| OrderID 🔍 | Customer 🔍 | Products 🔍 | Total Sales |
| Totals | | | 255 |
| 201 | 1 Chain,Mudguard,Seat | | 110 |
| 202 | 2 Basket,Gloves | | 75 |
| 203 | 3 Helmet | | 70 |

8. As you can see, all the products for a particular `OrderID` value are stringed together in a single cell and the sales figures are the aggregated figures for each `OrderID` value.

## How it works...

The `Concat()` function gives us the aggregated string concatenation of all the product values separated by the , delimiter. The `Concat()` function is an aggregation function and hence needs to be used with `AGGR` in order to be used as a dimension. For the sake of our dimension, the products are grouped by the `OrderID`.

The same functionality could have been achieved by defining products within a calculation in a measure as follows:

`Concat(DISTINCT Product,',')`

But by doing so, we won't be able to select the products for a particular `OrderID` value inside the table.

When we use the calculated dimension, we get the advantage of selecting all the products for the `OrderID` value in a single go by selecting a cell in the products column.

## There's more...

The `Concat()` function can also be used in the script along with the `Group By` clause.

## See also

> ▸  Using the `Fractile()` function to generate quartiles

# Using the Minstring() function to calculate the age of the oldest case in a queue

Support centers for any organization, log several customer cases during the day. These cases are sometimes tagged with a specific status such as *contact*, *review*, and so on. Each case goes through different statuses in the workflow until it reaches *closed* or *sign off* in the queue. The following example calculates the number of cases in each status of the workflow and then makes use of the `Minstring()` function to calculate the number of days passed since the oldest case logged for a particular status.

## Getting ready

Load the following script which gives information on the cases logged at a debt collection agency:

```
LET vToday=num(today());
Case:
LOAD  CaseID ,DATE(Date#( DateLogged,'DD/MM/YYYY')) as DateLogged,
Status INLINE [
CaseID,DateLogged,Status
101,01/01/2002,Advice
101,25/04/2002,Contact
101,21/06/2003,Creditors Meeting
101,24/06/2003,Draft Allocation
101,30/06/2003,Sign off
102,18/10/2009,Contact
102,28/10/2009,Advice
102,11/02/2010,Creditors Meeting
102,20/03/2010,Draft Allocation
102,30/06/2010,Review
103,11/02/2013,New Business
103,19/06/2013,Draft Allocation
104,30/06/2010,New Business
105,30/06/2010,Contact
105,11/02/2013,New Business
106,19/06/2013,Drafting
106,30/06/2010,Advice
];
```

## How to do it...

1. Drag the Table object onto the sheet from the Assets panel on the left. Name it `Oldest case in Queue (in days)`.

2. Add **Status** as the dimension.

3. Next, add the following expression as the first measure and label it `Case Volume`:

    `Count(CaseID)`

4. Add the following expression as the second measure and label it `Oldest item in Queue (in Days)`:

    ```
    Num($(vToday)-(MinString({$<DateLogged=>}
      [DateLogged])),'#,##0')
    ```

5. Under **Sorting**, promote **Status** to the top.

6. Under **Appearance**, click on **Presentation** and uncheck **Totals**.

7. Click on [🖉 **Done**] when finished.

8. The resulting table should look like the following screenshot. The figures you get for the **Oldest Item in Queue** table may be different, as the calculation is based on today's date, which will be different in your case:

| Oldest case in Queue (in days)' | | |
|---|---|---|
| Status 🔍 | Case Volume | Oldest Item in Queue in Days |
| Advice | 3 | 4,951 |
| Contact | 3 | 4,837 |
| Creditors Meeting | 2 | 4,415 |
| Draft Allocation | 3 | 4,412 |
| Drafting | 1 | 764 |
| New Business | 3 | 1,849 |
| Review | 1 | 1,849 |
| Sign off | 1 | 4,406 |

## How it works...

Today's date is stored in a number format in the variable `vToday()`. The `MinString()` function finds the oldest value in the `DateLogged` field from the total number of cases for each status. Next, we take a difference between `Today()` and the minimum date for each status to get the number of days for the oldest case.

## There's more...

By making use of the `Peek()` and `Previous()` functions and using the correct sort order during load, we can determine the case volume for each change of status. For example, *count of cases* that went from *advice* to *contact*, *contact* to *creditors meeting*, and so on.

## See also

▶ *Using the RangeSum() function to plot cumulative figures in trendline charts*

# Using the Rangesum() function to plot cumulative figures in trendline charts

The charts in Qlik Sense don't provide the user with the in-built functionality to calculate the cumulative totals, as is the case with QlikView. In order to achieve the cumulative totals in a trendline chart, we make use of the `RangeSum()` function.

## Getting ready

Load the following script that gives information of monthly sales figures for 2 years:

```
Sales:
LOAD
Month(Date#(Month,'MMM')) as Month,
Year,
Sales
INLINE [
Month,Year,Sales
Jan,2014,1000
Feb,2014,1520
Mar,2014,1600
Apr,2014,3000
May,2014,2500
Jun,2014,4500
Jul,2014,6000
Aug,2014,6500
Sep,2014,7800
Oct,2014,6800
Nov,2014,3000
Dec,2014,2500
Jan,2015,750
Feb,2015,1200
```

```
Mar,2015,800
Apr,2015,600
May,2015,2100
Jun,2015,3500
Jul,2015,4700
];
```

## How to do it...

1. Click on **App overview** under the Navigation dropdown and create a new sheet.

2. Drag across the 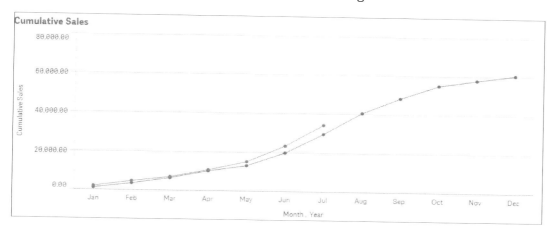 Line chart object from the Assets panel on the sheet and name it Cumulative Sales.

3. Add **Year** and **Month** as the dimensions.

4. Next, add the following measure and label it Cumulative Sales:

   RANGESUM(ABOVE(TOTAL Sum(Sales),0, ROWNO(TOTAL)))

5. Save the application and click on **Done**.

6. The final trendline chart should look like the following:

## How it works...

There are three arguments defined in the syntax used for the Above() function:

- ▶ Expression = Sum(Sales)

- ▶ Offset = '0'

  Since this is zero, the function evaluates the expression on the current row.

- ▸  `Count = RowNo(Total)`

  The third argument tells the `Above()` function to evaluate the expression over a range of values. In this case, because we are specifying a total inside the `Rowno()` function, the result would be the number of the row the user is currently on.

The `Above()` function will return a range of values. Hence we will use the `RangeSum()` function to sum up all the values.

## See also

- ▸  Using the `FirstSortedValue()` *function to identify the median in a quartile range*

# Using the Fractile() function to generate quartiles

Qlik Sense provides a host of statistical functions that can be put to effective use based on requirements in user reports. At a recent implementation, one of the requirements that popped out was to divide the data values into four quartiles. Quartiles are equivalent to percentiles which divide the data into four groups.

The first quartile is determined by every value which is equal to and less than the 25th percentile. The second quartile is determined by every value which is between the 25th and the 50th percentile. The third quartile is determined by every value which is between the 50th and the 75th percentile. The fourth quartile will be all the data values above and beyond the value of 75th percentile.

In order to generate quartiles in Qlik Sense, we make use of the `Fractile()` function. The following recipe explains the process.

## Getting ready

For the sake of this recipe we create a hypothetical situation and make use of an inline data load which gives a case level information for an insurance company. Load the following script in Qlik Sense:

```
Case:
LOAD * INLINE [
CaseID,Value,Status
101,1500,Active
102,1800,Active
103,800,Closed
104,2590,Closed
105,3500,Closed
```

```
106,1200,Active
107,5600,Active
108,8000,Closed
109,5960,Closed
110,5000,Active
111,4000,Active
112,2500,Active
];
```

## How to do it...

1. Click on **App overview** under the Navigation dropdown and create a new sheet.

2. Enter the Edit mode by clicking on [✏ Edit].

3. Drag the Table object on to the sheet.

4. Add the following calculated dimension and label it `Quartile`:

   ```
   =If (Value <= Fractile (TOTAL Value, 0.25), 'Quartile 1',
    If (Value <= Fractile (TOTAL Value, 0.50), 'Quartile 2',
    If (Value <= Fractile (TOTAL Value, 0.75),'Quartile 3',
    'Quartile 4')))
   ```

5. Add second dimension `CaseID`.

6. Add the following measure and label it `Value`:

   `Sum (Value)`

7. Under **Sorting**, promote `Value` to the top and sort it as numeric descending.

8. The resultant table would be as follows:

| Quartiles 🔍 | CaseID 🔍 | Value |
|---|---|---|
| **Totals** | | **42450** |
| Quartile 4 | 108 | 8000 |
| Quartile 4 | 109 | 5960 |
| Quartile 4 | 107 | 5600 |
| Quartile 3 | 110 | 5000 |
| Quartile 3 | 111 | 4000 |
| Quartile 3 | 105 | 3500 |
| Quartile 2 | 104 | 2590 |
| Quartile 2 | 112 | 2500 |
| Quartile 2 | 102 | 1800 |
| Quartile 1 | 101 | 1500 |
| Quartile 1 | 106 | 1200 |
| Quartile 1 | 103 | 800 |

9. As seen in the preceding screenshot, each `CaseID` value is now grouped under the Quartile.

## How it works...

The `Fractile ()` function finds the value corresponding to the stated quartile in the range of the data values given by the expression. For example, a `Fractile (TOTAL Value, 0.25)` works in the following way.

A value corresponding to the 25th percentile is calculated. The total qualifier disregards the chart dimensions.

In our calculated dimension, every `CaseID` having the value below the 25th percentile mark is tagged as *Quartile 1*, between 25th and 50th as *Quartile 2*, and so on.

## There's more...

We can make use of a distinct qualifier inside the `Fractile()` function. In such a case, only the unique values of the field `Value` are evaluated.

## See also

> ▸ *Using the FirstSortedValue() function to identify the median in a quartile range*

# Using the FirstSortedValue() function to identify the median in a quartile range

Our next task is to find a claim corresponding to the median value in each quartile. A median is nothing but a value corresponding to the 50th percentile. We can achieve this using the `FirstSortedvalue()` and `median()` functions.

## Getting ready

Continue with the same application as in the preceding recipe.

## How to do it...

1. Go to the Edit mode by clicking on **Edit**.
2. Select the table we created just now in the preceding recipe.

3. Edit the **CaseID** dimension and put in the following calculation:

```
=if(Match(CaseID,
'$(=FirstSortedValue(distinct{<Value={"<=$(=Median({<Value=
  {'>=$(=fractile(Value, 0))<=$(=Fractile(Value, 0.25))'}>}
  Value))"}>} CaseID, -Value))',
'$(=FirstSortedValue(distinct{<Value={"<=$(=Median({<Value=
  {'>$(=fractile(Value, 0.25))<=$(=fractile(Value,
  0.5))'}>} Value))"}>} CaseID, -Value))',
'$(=FirstSortedValue(distinct{<Value={"<=$(=Median({<Value=
  {'>$(=fractile(Value, 0.5))<=$(=fractile(Value,
  0.75))'}>} Value))"}>} CaseID, -Value))',
'$(=FirstSortedValue(distinct{<Value={"<=$(=Median({<Value=
  {'>$(=fractile(Value, 0.75))<=$(=fractile(Value, 1))'}>}
  Value))"}>} CaseID, -Value))'
),
CaseID,
Null()
)
```

4. Uncheck **Show Null Values** for **CaseID**.

5. The resultant table will look like this:

| Quartiles 🔍 | CaseID 🔍 | Value |
|---|---|---|
| Totals | | 13660 |
| Quartile 4 | 109 | 5960 |
| Quartile 3 | 111 | 4000 |
| Quartile 2 | 112 | 2500 |
| Quartile 1 | 106 | 1200 |

6. As you can see, every quartile is now showing only the claim corresponding to the median value in each quartile.

## How it works...

The calculated dimension for `CaseID` gives us the claims corresponding to the median values in each quartile. As you can see, a `Match()` function is being used to match the `CaseID` with each of the four expressions within.

Let's decipher the first expression inside the `Match()` function:

```
'$(=FirstSortedValue(distinct
{<Value={"<=$(=Median({<Value={'>=$(=fractile(Value,
   0))<=$(=fractile(Value, 0.25))'}>} Value))"}>} CaseID, -Value))'
```

The details of the expressions are as follows:

▸ The innermost set gives us the range of values which are between the 0th quartile value and the 25th Quartile value

▸ The `Median()` function then gives us the value which lies at the median of this range

▸ The `FirstSortedvalue()` returns the value of the output field (`CaseID`) based on the sorted values of the value field

In situations where the number of claims in any quartile is an even number, there will be two claims which will correspond to the median values. In such a scenario, we want to select only the claim which is higher in the sorting order. Hence, we use a `-Value` as the sort weight.

## There's more...

Similar to medians, we can derive the quartiles within quartiles using the `Fractile()` function.

## See also

▸ *Using the Fractile() function to generate quartiles*

# Using the Declare and Derive functions to generate Calendar fields

Defining a Master Calendar in Qlik Sense is a common requirement and can be done using the `Time` and `Date` functions. With Sense, Qlik has introduced the `Declare` and `Derive` functions, which make it easier to create the `Calendar` definition. This is still not commonly used, as most Qlik Sense developers stick to their old Calendar scripts, and there is nothing wrong with that. However, these functions are worth exploring.

## Getting ready

Load the following part of the script that gives information on organization sales into the Qlik Sense application:

```
OrgSales:
LOAD Product, OrderNo ,DATE(Date#( InvoiceDate,'DD/MM/YYYY')) as
   InvoiceDate,
Sales INLINE [
InvoiceDate,Product,OrderNo,Sales
1/1/2013,Chains,101,5500
8/2/2014,Seats,101,4800
3/3/2014,Brake Oil,102,6500
9/5/2015,Helmets,104,4500
];
```

## How to do it...

Using the `INLINE` table specified in the preceding code, we will generate a Master Calendar. We will generate the fields and `Group` definition using the `Declare` function.

1.  In the data load editor, type in the following script:

    ```
    Calendar:
    Declare Field Definition Tagged '$date'
    Parameters
        first_month_of_year=1
     Fields
           Year($1)  as Year Tagged '$year',
            Month($1) as Month Tagged '$month',
            Date($1) as Date Tagged '$date',
            Week($1,first_month_of_year) as Week Tagged '$week'

        Groups
        Year,Month,Date type collection as YearMonthDate;
    ```

2.  Once the `Calendar` definition is created, it needs to be linked back to the date field using the `Derive` function. Insert the following statement in the script and reload the application:

    ```
    Derive Fields from Fields InvoiceDate using Calendar;
    ```

3.  On a new sheet, click on edit and then on the Fields tab ▤ on the Assets panel to the left. At the bottom of the panel you will see there is a new tab for the time and date functions. Once you expand this, you should be able to see all the fields we created under the `Declare` statement.

## How it works...

The `Declare` function is used to create the `Calendar` definition and tag it to `$date`. The `Calendar` definition is then used to derive related dimensions such as **Year**, **Month**, **Week**, and so on.

The parameter `first_month_of_year` indicates what the first month of the year should be. It contains comma-separated values, but it is optional and can be skipped if needed.

Next, we define the fields we want to generate in the `Calendar` table. The `$1` represents the data field from which the date field will be generated, which is `InvoiceDate` in our case.

When the field definition is used, a comma-separated list of fields is generated. The `Derive` function is used in order to generate the derived fields such as **Year**, **Month**, and so on from the `InvoiceDate` field. The groups are defined at the end of the script that creates a drilldown group for **Year**, **Month**, and **Date**.

## There's more...

The `Derive` function can be used to link back the `Calendar` to multiple dates separated by a comma. For example, "derive fields from fields `InvoiceDate`, `ShippingDate` using `Calendar`".

Similar to the resident load, a `Calendar` table can be loaded again in the script. We can change the parameter value of the first month of the year to `3`. The earlier value of the parameter is overridden by doing this. This is achieved with the following commands:

```
MyCalendar:
DECLARE FIELD DEFINITION USING Calendar WITH
  first_month_of_year=3;
DERIVE FIELDS FROM FIELDS InvoiceDate USING MyCalendar;
```

## See also

> ▶  *Using the Peek() function to create a currency Exchange Rate Calendar*

# Setting up a moving annual total figure

A **moving annual total** (**MAT**) is the total value of a variable, such as sales figures for a product, over the course of the previous 12 months. This is a rolling yearly sum, so it changes at the end of each month with data from the new month added to the total and data from the first month of the period taken away read more about moving annual total (MAT), at `http://www.pmlive.com/intelligence/healthcare_glossary_211509/Terms/m/moving_annual_total_mat`.

## Getting ready

We are going to make use of variables in this recipe. We will define three variables in the script: `vMonthFormat`, `vRolling12Months`, and `vMaxMonth`.

Load the following script into your Qlik Sense application:

```
LET vMonthFormat = 'MMM-YYYY';
LET v12MonthsBack = 'Date(AddMonths(max([MonthYear]), -
   12),$(vMonthFormat))';
LET vMaxMonth='Date(max([MonthYear]),$(vMonthFormat))';


Sales:
LOAD
Date(Date#(MonthYear, 'MMMYYYY'), 'MMM-YYYY') as MonthYear,
Month(Date#(MonthYear, 'MMMYYYY')) as Month,
Year(Date#(MonthYear, 'MMMYYYY')) as Year,
Sales INLINE [

MonthYear, Sales
Jan2014, 1000
Feb2014, 1520
Mar2014, 1600
Apr2014, 3000
May2014, 2500
Jun2014, 4500
Jul2014, 6000
Aug2014, 6500
Sep2014, 7800
Oct2014, 6800
Nov2014, 3000
Dec2014, 2500
Jan2015, 750
Feb2015, 1200
Mar2015, 800
Apr2015, 600
May2015, 2100
Jun2015, 3500
Jul2015, 4700
Aug2015, 2100
Sep2015, 3500
Oct2015, 4700
];
```

```
FOR vMonth = 0 to 11
MATMonthYear:
LOAD
[MonthYear],
Date(AddMonths([MonthYear], $(vMonth)),'$(vMonthFormat)') as [MAT
   MonthYear]
RESIDENT Sales
WHERE AddMonths([MonthYear], $(vMonth)) < today()
;
next
```

## How to do it...

1. Once the data is loaded, open the **App overview** window and create a new sheet.

2. Enter the Edit mode by clicking on [ ✎ **Edit** ].

3. Drag across the [ ⎍ Line chart ] object from the Assets panel on the sheet.

4. Name it `Moving Annual Total`.

5. Add [MAT MonthYear] as the dimension.

6. Next, add the following measure and label it MAT Sales:

   ```
   SUM({<[MAT
      MonthYear]={">=$(vRolling12Months)<=
      $(vMaxMonth)"}>}Sales)
   ```

7. Save the application and click on [ ✎ **Done** ].

8. Under **Appearance**, select the chart style as [📈 Area].

9. Check the **Show Data** points.

10. Switch on the **Value Labels** options to show values on each data point.

11. The final trendline chart should look like this:

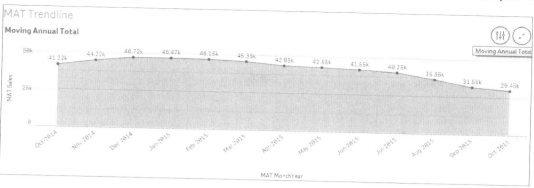

## How it works...

The **Moving Annual Total** curve helps in smoothing out the spikes that occur in a single month by making use of the annual totals. This is achieved by calculating the rolling 12 months accumulated sales data for each data point.

We create a **MATMonthYear** field. You will notice that when we select any month and year value in this field, it associates the field value to the current MonthYear and the 11 MonthYears prior to the current, in the MonthYear field.

In the **MAT Sales** expression, we make sure that the rolling 12 months are always shown in the chart. This is achieved by restricting the **MATMonthYear** values shown in the chart between the vRolling12Months and the vMaxMonth variables.

Selecting any **MATMonthYear** will result in the trendline chart populating the MAT figures for the selected month and 11 months prior to that.

## There's more...

There is a similar concept known as cumulative sums, which we discussed in the recipe *Using the Rangesum() function to plot cumulative figures in trendline charts*. However, there is a glaring difference between the two. While cumulative takes into consideration all the previous months and years to the current, a Moving Annual Total will always consider the previous 12 months. In a way it is a rolling 12 month sum at any given point of time.

## See also

- ▸  *Using the Rangesum() function to plot cumulative figures in trendline charts*

# Using the For Each loop to extract files from a folder

Picture a scenario where the month end sales data in an organization is stored in a folder on the network from where it needs to be picked up for reporting purposes.

Control statements such as *For Each next* can be used in Qlik Sense as an approach towards script iteration. The following recipe deals with extracting files in Qlik Sense from a folder, processing them to create QVD files and then transferring the source files to another folder. In the process, we will also deal with the incremental update of the QVD.

## Getting ready

This recipe requires the Legacy mode to be activated. The steps are as follows:

1. To activate the Legacy mode, open the `Settings.ini` file under `C:\Users\<username>\Documents\Qlik\Sense`.

2. Change the value of the `StandardReload` parameter from `1` to `0`.

3. For this recipe, we make use of four Excel files: `January.xlsx`, `February.xlsx`, `March.xlsx`, and `April.xlsx`. These files are provided with the chapter and can be downloaded from the Packt Publishing website.

4. Save the file `January.xlsx` under `c:\QlikSense`. If you are not able to write to this location, then you may change the storage location for the file. Note that in this case you will have to make relevant changes in the file location paths for the load script discussed in the *How to do it...* section for this recipe.

5. Create another folder named `Processed` inside the `QlikSense` folder we created in step 1. The path for the folder would be `c:\QlikSense\Processed`.

6. Create a third folder named `QVD` inside the `QlikSense` folder created in step 1. The path for the folder would be `c:\QlikSense\QVD`.

## How to do it...

1. Create a new Qlik Sense application.

2. Open the data load editor.

3. Load the following script:

```
For each File in filelist ('C:\QlikSense\*.xlsx')

ProdSales:
LOAD
```

```
   left(FileBaseName(),18) AS ProdSalesFileName,
filename() as FileName,
 [Product],
[Sales]
FROM [$(File)]
(ooxml, embedded labels, table is Sheet1)
WHERE Sales >250000;


Execute cmd.exe /C move "$(File)" "C:\QlikSense\Processed";


next File


SET rowCount = 0;
LET rowCount = NoOfRows('ProdSales');


IF rowCount > 0 AND Alt(FileSize('C:\ QlikSense
  \QVD\ProdSales.QVD'),0) > 0 THEN
Concatenate(ProdSales)


LOAD * FROM C:\\QlikSense\QVD\ProdSales.QVD (qvd);


STORE ProdSales INTO C:\QlikSense\QVD\ProdSales.QVD;


ELSE


STORE ProdSales INTO C:\QlikSense\QVD\ProdSales.QVD;


END IF


DROP TABLE ProdSales;


LOAD * FROM C:\QlikSense\QVD\ProdSales.QVD (qvd);
```

4. Now, add the remaining three Excel files, that is, `February.xlsx`, `March.xlsx`, and `April.xlsx`, to the source location; in the case of this recipe, it is `c:\QlikSense`.

5. Load the script again. You will notice that all the files have been processed and moved to the processed folder. At the same time, the new data is appended to the `ProdSales.QVD` file.

6. In order to test the data loaded into the QVD, go to **App overview** and create a new sheet.

7. Drag a table object onto the sheet.

8. Add **ProdSalesFileName** as the first dimension and label it `Month`.

9. Add **Product** as second dimension.

10. Add the following expression and label it as `Sales`:

    ```
    Sum(Sales)
    ```

11. The resultant table would look like the following, with each month showing records only with `Sales >250000`:

| Month | Product | Sales |
|---|---|---|
| **Totals** | | **6882967** |
| April | 2589 | 589686 |
| April | 4545 | 526352 |
| April | 7852 | 323256 |
| February | 2563 | 658968 |
| February | 2589 | 489868 |
| February | 7852 | 451185 |
| January | 4545 | 658936 |
| January | 7852 | 458788 |
| January | 2563 | 456698 |
| January | 4568 | 452658 |
| January | 7856 | 452563 |

## How it works...

The `for each next` loop iterates through each file in the `Source` folder and processes it to pick up records with sales greater than 250,000. Once processed, the files are transferred to the processed folder using the command prompt.

The `if` condition checks for the row count of the processed file. If it is greater than zero then the file is concatenated to the existing `ProdSales.QVD` file. The `LOAD` statement inside the `if` condition has a **WHERE** not exists clause which makes sure to append only new files to the QVD.

# Using the Peek() function to create a currency Exchange Rate Calendar

Organizations dealing in multiple currencies may use a web service to extract the exchange rates. They may even store the currency exchange rates in Excel files or sometimes in a database table. The exchange rates for any currency may be stored only for each `RateStartDate` that is for the day when the rate changes its value. However, for our reporting purposes we need exchange rates for each day and not just for the day when the rate changes its value. For this purpose, it is beneficial to create an Exchange Rate Calendar.

## Getting ready

Create a new Qlik Sense application and load the following script into your Qlik Sense application:

```
ExchangeRatetemp:
LOAD FromCurrency,ExchangeRate,
DATE(Date#(RateStartDate,'DD/MM/YYYY')) as RateStartDate INLINE [
FromCurrency, ExchangeRate, RateStartDate
EUR,0.687,01/08/2012
EUR,0.757,02/09/2012
EUR,0.74,08/09/2013
EUR,1.10,24/10/2014
SGD,0.52,01/08/2012
SGD,0.68,27/02/2014
SGD,0.88,28/03/2015
USD,0.75,14/12/2013
USD,0.77,16/01/2014
USD,0.85,26/06/2015
];
```

## How to do it...

We will now generate the end dates for each currency exchange rate:

1. Load the following script to generate the `RateEndDate` for each exchange rate:

```
ExchangeRate:
LOAD
FromCurrency,
ExchangeRate,
Date (RateStartDate) AS RateStartDate,
If (FromCurrency=Peek (FromCurrency), Date (Peek
   (RateStartDate)-1), Today ()) AS RateEndDate
RESIDENT
ExchangeRatetemp
ORDER BY FromCurrency, RateStartDate DESC;

DROP TABLE ExchangeRatetemp;
```

2. Go to the **App overview** window and open a new sheet.

3. Enter the Edit mode by clicking on 🖉 **Edit**.

4. Drag the Table object onto the screen and add all the four dimensions to it. Promote **RateStartDate** to the top of the sorting order and set the sort order as numeric ascending.

5. The result would be as follows:

| FromCurrency | ExchangeRate | RateStartDate | RateEndDate |
|---|---|---|---|
| EUR | 0.687 | 01/08/2012 | 01/09/2012 |
| EUR | 0.757 | 02/09/2012 | 07/09/2013 |
| EUR | 0.74 | 08/09/2013 | 23/10/2014 |
| EUR | 1.10 | 24/10/2014 | 27/07/2015 |
| SGD | 0.52 | 01/08/2012 | 26/02/2014 |
| SGD | 0.68 | 27/02/2014 | 27/03/2015 |
| SGD | 0.88 | 28/03/2015 | 27/07/2015 |
| USD | 0.75 | 14/12/2013 | 15/01/2014 |
| USD | 0.77 | 16/01/2014 | 25/06/2015 |
| USD | 0.85 | 26/06/2015 | 27/07/2015 |

6. As we can see, every record for a currency now has a rate end date.

7. We will now use the `RateStartDate` and `RateEndDate` fields as our base dates for the Exchange Rate Calendar.

8. Now, copy and paste the following script after the `DROP TABLE ExchangeRatetemp` statement:

```
//--------------------------------------------------
// Generate calendar dates
//--------------------------------------------------

LET ExStartDate = Num(Peek('RateStartDate', -1,
  ExchangeRate));
LET ExEndDate = Num(Peek('RateEndDate', 0, ExchangeRate));

ExchangeRateCalendar:
LOAD
Date($(ExStartDate) + RecNo() - 1) AS ExchangeRateDate
AUTOGENERATE
($(ExEndDate) - $( ExStartDate) + 1);


//--------------------------------------------------
// INTERVAL MATCH JOIN the month records to the calendar
// table
//--------------------------------------------------

LEFT JOIN (ExchangeRateCalendar)
```

```
INTERVALMATCH (ExchangeRateDate)
LOAD
RateStartDate,
RateEndDate
RESIDENT
ExchangeRate;

LEFT JOIN (ExchangeRateCalendar)
LOAD * RESIDENT ExchangeRate;

DROP TABLE ExchangeRate;

ExchangeRate:
LOAD
FromCurrency,
ExchangeRateDate,
ExchangeRate
RESIDENT
ExchangeRateCalendar;

DROP TABLE ExchangeRateCalendar;
```

9. Again create a Table object on the sheet and get all the dimensions from the `ExchangeRate` table.

10. We will have exchange rates for each of the missing dates as well as shown in the following screenshot:

| FromCurrency | ExchangeRate | ExchangeRateDate |
|---|---|---|
| EUR | 0.74 | 14/12/2013 |
| EUR | 0.74 | 15/12/2013 |
| EUR | 0.74 | 16/12/2013 |
| EUR | 0.74 | 17/12/2013 |
| EUR | 0.74 | 18/12/2013 |
| EUR | 0.74 | 19/12/2013 |
| EUR | 0.74 | 20/12/2013 |
| EUR | 0.74 | 21/12/2013 |
| EUR | 0.74 | 22/12/2013 |
| EUR | 0.74 | 23/12/2013 |
| EUR | 0.74 | 24/12/2013 |
| EUR | 0.74 | 25/12/2013 |
| EUR | 0.74 | 26/12/2013 |
| EUR | 0.74 | 27/12/2013 |

## How it works...

The main purpose of creating this exchange rate calendar is to tag the exchange rates to every missing date in the range.

The initial data only comes with the rate start dates. So we create a rate end date for each exchange rate using the `Peek()` function. The `Peek()` function checks for the last read record for `FromCurrency` and if it matches, it generates a rate end date of `current RateStartDate -1`. If `FromCurrency` doesn't match, then the rate end date is set to today's date.

Using these start and end dates, the calendar is generated.

## There's more...

The exchange rate calendar generated in the preceding recipe can be set for a daily update and stored in a QVD file that can then be used in any Qlik Sense application involving monetary analysis.

## See also

> ▸ *Using the Peek() function to create a Trial Balance sheet*

# Using the Peek() function to create a Trial Balance sheet

A Trial Balance sheet captures the activity across different accounts of a company with regards to the opening and closing balances. The following recipe focuses on creation of a trial balance sheet in Qlik Sense.

## Getting ready

The recipe will make use of the `TrialBalance.xlsx` file, which can be downloaded from the Packt Publishing website.

Store the file on your system at the following location `C:/QlikSense`.

## How to do it...

1. Create a folder connection to the `Trial Balance.xlsx` file. Name it `QlikSenseCookBook _TB`.

2. Load the data from the `TrialBalance.xlsx` file in the Qlik Sense file. We need to make use of the cross table functionality to load the data in a proper format:

```
Let vMaxMonth=Max(Month);

TrialBalancetemp:
CrossTable(Month, Amount, 4)
LOAD [Company Number],
   [Account Number],
   [Year],
     Forwarded,
   [January],
   [February],
   [March],
   [April],
   [May],
   [June],
   [July],
   [August],
   [September],
   [October],
   [November],
   [December]
FROM [lib://QlikSenseCookBook_TB/Trial Balance.xlsx]
(ooxml, embedded labels, table is Sheet1);
```

3. Next, we will generate the `Month` and the `MonthYear` field in a resident load. Copy and paste the following script:

```
TrialBalancetemp1:
NoConcatenate LOAD
[Company Number],
[Account Number],
 Forwarded,
Year,
Month(Date#(Month,'MMM')) as Month,
Date(MakeDate(Year, Month(Date#(Month,'MMM'))), 'MMM YYYY')
   as MonthYear,
Amount
Resident TrialBalancetemp;
DROP Table TrialBalancetemp;
```

4. The final step is to create the `Opening Balance` and `Closing Balance` fields using the `Peek()` function. Copy and paste the following script in the editor:

```
TrialBalance:
NoConcatenate LOAD
CompanyAccountKey,
[Company Number],
[Account Number],
MonthYear,
Year,
Month,
Amount,
if(Rowno() = 1 OR CompanyAccountKey <>
Peek(CompanyAccountKey), Forwarded, Peek(Closing)) as
Opening,
    if(Rowno() = 1 OR CompanyAccountKey <>
    Peek(CompanyAccountKey), Forwarded + Amount,
    Peek(Closing) + Amount) as Closing
;
NoConcatenate LOAD
[Company Number] & '_' & [Account Number] as
CompanyAccountKey,
[Company Number],
[Account Number],
Year,
Month,
MonthYear,
Forwarded,
Amount
Resident TrialBalancetemp1
Order By [Company Number], [Account Number], MonthYear;
DROP Table TrialBalancetemp1;
```

5. Load the data and save the file. Open **App overview** by clicking on the Navigation dropdown ⊘▾ at the top-left corner.

6. Add the Table object to the sheet.

7. Add **MonthYear**, **Company Number**, and **Account Number** as dimensions.

8. Next, we will add the expressions for measures. We specify a range of months in the set analysis expression. When we define the range, it is enclosed within double quotes (" "). If you try to copy this expression and paste it in the Qlik Sense expression editor, sometimes the double quotes are not copied in the correct format. If the format for the quotes is incorrect, the `vMaxMonth` variable is highlighted in purple. In this case, the user must make sure that a proper format of double quotes is in place.

9. Add the first expression to the table and label it `Opening`:

   `Sum({<Month={"<=$(vMaxMonth)"}>} Opening)`

10. Add the second expression to the table and label it `Amount`:

    `Sum({<Month={"<=$(vMaxMonth)"}>} Amount)`

11. Add the third expression to the table and label it `Closing`:

    `Sum({<Month={"<=$(vMaxMonth)"}>} Closing)`

12. Under **Sorting**, promote **Account Number** to the top and set the sort order as numerically ascending.

13. Promote **Company Number** to the second position in sorting and set the sort order as numerically ascending.

14. The final table report will look like this:

TrialBalance

| MonthYear | Company Number | Account Number | Opening | Amount | Closing |
|---|---|---|---|---|---|
| **Totals** | | | **151000** | **9000** | **160000** |
| Jan 2015 | 1 | 1001 | 10000 | 1000 | 11000 |
| Feb 2015 | 1 | 1001 | 11000 | 1000 | 12000 |
| Mar 2015 | 1 | 1001 | 12000 | 1000 | 13000 |
| Apr 2015 | 1 | 1001 | 13000 | -1000 | 12000 |
| May 2015 | 1 | 1001 | 12000 | 1000 | 13000 |
| Jun 2015 | 1 | 1001 | 13000 | 1000 | 14000 |
| Jul 2015 | 1 | 1001 | 14000 | 1000 | 15000 |
| Aug 2015 | 1 | 1001 | 15000 | 1000 | 16000 |
| Sep 2015 | 1 | 1001 | 16000 | 1000 | 17000 |
| Oct 2015 | 1 | 1001 | 17000 | 1000 | 18000 |
| Nov 2015 | 1 | 1001 | 18000 | 1000 | 19000 |

## How it works...

The script uses a `rowno()` function and a `Peek()` function to calculate the **Opening** and **Closing** balances.

The `rowno()` function determines the position of the current row. If we are at the first row, then the **Forwarded Amount** is taken as the opening balance. If the company and account have changed, then we use the `Peek()` function to determine the previous closing balance, which is taken as the opening balance.

Similarly, if we are at the first row, then the **Forwarded Amount** + **Amount** added for the particular month, is taken as the closing balance. If the company and account have changed, then we use the `Peek()` function to determine the previous closing balance and add this value to the amount to get the final closing balance.

## See also

▶ *Using the Peek() function to create a currency Exchange Rate Calendar*

# 6
# Set Analysis

In this chapter, we will focus on the concept of Set Analysis and its use in Qlik Sense. We will cover the following topics:

- ▶ Cracking the syntax for Set Analysis
- ▶ Using flags in Set Analysis
- ▶ Using the = sign with variables in Set Analysis
- ▶ Point in time using Set Analysis
- ▶ Using comparison sets in Set Analysis
- ▶ Using embedded functions in Set Analysis
- ▶ Creating a multi-measure expression in Set Analysis
- ▶ Using search strings inside a set modifier
- ▶ Capturing a list of field values using a `concat()` function in Set Analysis
- ▶ Using the element functions `P()` and `E()` in Set Analysis

## Introduction

I will say it outright that Set Analysis is one of the most important technical features of Qlik solutions. It allows you to do things dynamically that just won't be possible with the default selections you have made. Set analysis can be termed as **Selection analysis**. The user tells Qlik Sense what set of records need to be picked for calculation which is similar to making a selection from a Filter pane or active objects. The only difference is that you define the selection inside the calculation. So that the expression can still look at the records you specified inside the Set Analysis expression even if you clear all the default selections.

# Cracking the syntax for Set Analysis

Set Analysis is a very powerful concept in Qlik Sense. In very simple terms, each Set contains a "group" of selected dimensional values. The sets allow the users to create independent selections, other than the one being used in the active Qlik Sense objects. The aggregations inside the Set are compared with current selections to get the desired results.

 Any set that has been created in Qlik Sense only alters the context of the expression that uses it. Unless they are referencing label names inside the same visualization, all expressions using the set syntax are independent of each other. As such, basic expressions not using the Set Analysis will react to the normal selections made inside the Qlik Sense document.

A Set Analysis expression consists of three main parts:

1. Set identifiers for example $, 1, 1-$, and so on
2. Set operators
3. Set modifiers (optional)

The set expression is defined inside curly brackets { }. The set identifiers are separated from the modifiers by angular (< >) brackets.

Set identifiers define the relationship between the set expression and the field values or the expression that is being evaluated (Qlik, help).

The set modifier is made up of one or several field names, each followed by a selection that should be made on the field (Qlik, help).

For example, to compare the current year versus last year sales for three countries, we can write the following Set Analysis expression:

```
Sum({$<Year={2014,2015},Country={'USA', 'UK', 'GERMANY'}>}Sales)
```

## Getting ready

Load the following script that gives information on the Sales values for four customers:

```
Sales:
LOAD * INLINE [
Customer,Month,Volume,Sales
ABC,Jan,100,7500
DEF,Feb,200,8500
GHI,Mar,400,12000
JKL,Apr,100,4500
];
```

The following recipe will explain the basics of set expression. The aim is to retrieve customers with volumes greater than or equal to `200`.

## How to do it...

1. Drag across the Table object onto the Sheet from the Assets panel. Name it `Set Analysis`.

2. Add **Customer** as Dimension.

3. Add **Sum(Sales)** as the measure and label it as `Sales`.

4. In order to define the set, open the Expression editor window by clicking on the *fx* . button.

5. Start constructing the set expression by first inserting the curly brackets { } just before the word `Sales`.

6. Inside the curly bracket, put in the set identifier `$`.

7. Finally, we will define the set modifier. As mentioned earlier, the modifiers are separated from the identifier using angular brackets < >. Insert < > after the $ sign. Type in `Volume = {}` inside the angular brackets.

8. Inside the angular brackets after `Volume`, type in `>=200`. Note the double quotes.

9. The final Set Analysis expression will look similar to the following:

   `Sum({$<Volume ={">=200"}>} Sales)`

10. Click [ ✎ **Done** ] when finished.

11. The table should look similar to the following:

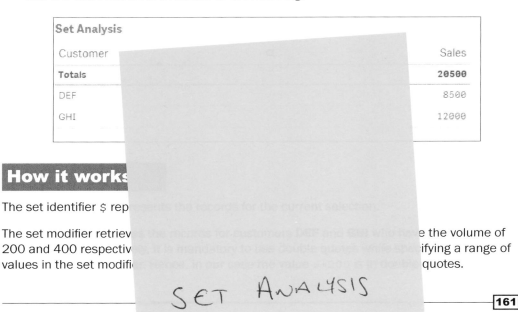

| Set Analysis | |
| --- | --- |
| Customer | Sales |
| Totals | 20500 |
| DEF | 8500 |
| GHI | 12000 |

## How it works

The set identifier $ rep[resents the records for the current selection].

The set modifier retriev[es the records for customers DEF and GHI who hav]e the volume of 200 and 400 respectiv[ely. It is mandatory to use double quotes while spec]ifying a range of values in the set modifi[er. Hence, in our case the value >=200 is in double] quotes.

SET ANALYSIS

## There's more...

A set modifier can consist of multiple field names with selections made on them. We can also exclude selections in a particular field by specifying the field name followed by an = sign. For example, if we want to exclude the month selection then our expression will become:

```
Sum({$<Month=,Volume ={">=200"}>} Sales)
```

## See also

▶ *Creating a multi-measure expression in Set Analysis*

# Using flags in Set Analysis

Set Analysis expressions tend to become overly complex when there are too many comparison sets and conditions put in place. In order to reduce the complexity, one can make use of the flags created in the script in the Set Analysis expression. The flags can be set up to be simple binary values, 0 and 1. Use of flags optimizes the performance of frontend calculations. The following recipe explores this possibility by creating flags in the script to identify the "On-time" and "Late" shipments.

## Getting ready

For the purpose of this recipe,we will be using an inline data load which contains shipment details for each customer. Load the following script within the Qlik Sense data load editor:

```
SalesTemp:
LOAD DATE(Date#(DeliveryDate,'DD/MM/YYYY')) AS DeliveryDate,
DATE(Date#(ShipmentDate,'DD/MM/YYYY')) AS ShipmentDate,
Invoiceno.,Customer,Month,Sales INLINE [
Invoiceno.,Customer,Month,DeliveryDate,ShipmentDate,Sales
101,ABC,Jan,01/01/2015,29/12/2014,10000
102,ABC,Feb,02/02/2015,25/01/2015,10000
103,ABC,Mar,03/03/2015,02/03/2015,12000
104,ABC,Apr,04/04/2015,24/01/2015,10000
105,DEF,Feb,03/02/2015,03/02/2015,25000
106,DEF,Mar,25/03/2015,21/03/2015,25000
107,DEF,Apr,18/04/2015,14/04/2015,25000
108,GHI,Jan,24/01/2015,18/01/2015,8500
109,GHI,Mar,14/03/2015,09/03/2015,7000
110,GHI,Jun,06/08/2015,07/06/2015,5000
];
```

```
Sales:
LOAD * ,
IF(num(DeliveryDate)-num(ShipmentDate)>=0 AND
Num(DeliveryDate)-num(ShipmentDate)<5 ,1,
IF(num(DeliveryDate)-num(ShipmentDate)>=5 AND
Num(DeliveryDate)-num(ShipmentDate)<25 ,2,3)) AS
   OntimeLateFlag
RESIDENT SalesTemp;
DROP TABLE SalesTemp;
```

## How to do it...

1. Drag across the Table object from the left-hand side Assets panel on to the sheet. Name it `Invoiced Sales`.

2. Add the following dimensions:

    ❑ `InvoiceNo`.

    ❑ `DeliveryDate`

    ❑ `ShipmentDate`

3. Add the following expression under data and label it as `Sales`:

   `Sum({$<OntimeLateFlag={1}>}Sales)`

4. Under **Sorting**, promote `Sales` to the top.

5. Click on **Save** and [ 🖉 **Done** ].

6. The resulting table on the screen should look similar to the following:

| Invoiced Sales | | | |
|---|---|---|---|
| Invoiceno. 🔍 | DeliveryDate 🔍 | ShipmentDate 🔍 | Sales |
| Totals | | | **97000** |
| 105 | 03/02/2015 | 03/02/2015 | 25000 |
| 106 | 25/03/2015 | 21/03/2015 | 25000 |
| 107 | 18/04/2015 | 14/04/2015 | 25000 |
| 103 | 03/03/2015 | 02/03/2015 | 12000 |
| 101 | 01/01/2015 | 29/12/2014 | 10000 |

7. Note that only the invoices with a delivery time of less than 5 days are shown in the preceding table.

## How it Works...

The calculation to identify the "On time" and "late" shipments is done in the script and it is executed only once. Every `OnTime` shipment is flagged as `1` and a slight delay as `2` and late as `3`. Use of these flags in the frontend objects will filter the data in the table accordingly.

## There's more...

In order to give a more meaningful representation to the flags in the frontend, we may use the dual function. A `Dual()` function combines a number and a string into a single record. The number representation of the record can be used to sort and also for calculation purposes, while the string value can be used for display purposes.

In order to do this:

1. Rename the `Sales` table to `SalesTemp1`.

2. Add the following `Resident` load:

```
Sales:
LOAD *,
IF(OntimeLateFlag =1, Dual('OnTime',1),
IF(OntimeLateFlag =2, Dual('SlightDelay',2),
   Dual('Late',3))) As Flag
RESIDENT SalesTemp1;
DROP Table SalesTemp1;
```

3. Save and reload the application.

4. In the frontend, drag across the Filter pane object and add the **OntimeLateFlag** and **Flag** dimension to it.

5. Note that every **OntimeLateFlag** value is now associated with text:

Using flags with a string format in Set Analysis expressions may not always be the most efficient way of optimizing the performance of the Qlik Sense objects. With a big data set, using a flag with a string representation in the expression does not offer a massive advantage as far as the performance standpoint is concerned. However, if we have binary flags `0` and `1` then multiplying these flags by the measures results in a faster performance in the user interface.

Hence, we conclude the following:

- To make selections in the application, use the `String` representation of flags in the Filter pane objects
- To calculate a condition inside a Set Analysis expression, use the numeric representation of flags

## See also

- *Using embedded functions in Set Analysis*

# Using the = sign with variables in Set Analysis

We can make use of variables and calculations in the set modifiers. The following recipe explains the syntax to use variables for comparison in sets and how to effectively use the = sign in the dollar sign expansions.

## Getting ready

For the purpose of this recipe, we will be using an inline data load which contain shipment details for each customer. Load the following script in the Qlik Sense data load editor. Make sure that the last record in this script has the `Month` set to today's month and the `DeliveryDate` set to today's date:

```
Let vToday=Today ();

Sales:
LOAD DATE(Date#(DeliveryDate, 'DD/MM/YYYY')) AS DeliveryDate,
DATE(Date#(ShipmentDate, 'DD/MM/YYYY')) AS ShipmentDate,
Customer,Month,Volume,Sales,Supplier
INLINE [
```

```
Customer,Month,DeliveryDate,ShipmentDate,Volume,Sales,Supplier
ABC,Jan,01/01/2015,29/12/2014,100,10000,DEF
ABC,Feb,02/02/2015,25/01/2015,100,10000,DEF
ABC,Mar,03/03/2015,02/03/2015,400,12000,DEF
ABC,Apr,04/04/2015,24/01/2015,100,10000,GHI
DEF,Feb,03/02/2015,03/02/2015,200,25000,GHI
DEF,Mar,25/03/2015,21/03/2015,300,25000,GHI
DEF,Apr,18/04/2015,14/04/2015,200,25000,ABC
GHI,Jan,24/01/2015,18/01/2015,200,8500,ABC
GHI,Mar,14/03/2015,09/03/2015,200,7000,ABC
GHI,Jun,06/08/2015,07/06/2015,200,5000,ABC
];
```

## How to do it...

1. Drag across a Table object from the Assets panel onto the sheet.
2. Add **Customer** as dimension.
3. Now add the following calculation as the measure and label it `Sales`:

   `Sum({$<DeliveryDate={'$(vToday)'}>}Sales)`

4. Click on **Save** and then `Done`.
5. The resultant table is similar to the following figure with only one record for customer **GHI**:

6. Next, update the `Sales` calculation as shown:

   `Sum({$<DeliveryDate={'$(TODAY())'}>}Sales)`

7. When you save this calculation, Qlik Sense won't be able to interpret the result and we will get the following output:

8. Tweak the sales calculation by adding a = sign in front of `TODAY()`:

```
Sum({$<DeliveryDate={'$(=TODAY())'}>}Sales)
```

9. The result will be as seen earlier with one record for the customer **GHI**.

## How it works...

We have defined the `vToday` variable in the script. This variable stores the values for today's date. When we use this variable inside the set modifier, we just use a simple `$` sign expansion.

The `vToday` variable is calculated before the script is executed. However, Qlik Sense fails to interpret the result when we use the `TODAY()` function inside the set modifier instead of `vToday`. The reason being that the `$` sign expansion needs to perform a calculation in the form of `TODAY()` and without the preceding = sign the date for today won't be calculated.

Hence, we proceed to `TODAY()` with the = sign. Once the = sign is in place, the sales for customers with today's delivery date are calculated.

If we are not using any calculation inside the set modifier then the variable can be defined with or without the = sign.

## See also

▸ *Point in time using Set Analysis*

# Point in time using Set Analysis

How is this month looking compared to the last? This is one of the most common questions asked in BI solutions. In this recipe, we will build two charts and both will compare one year to the other. The first chart expression will limit the range of data and make use of the **Year** dimension. The second chart will not use the **Year** dimension but will build the year comparison directly into the expression itself.

For the purpose of this recipe,we will make use of an inline data load which gives yearly sales information for different fruits. Load the following data into the data load editor:

```
Data:
LOAD * INLINE [
    Fruit, Year, Sales
    Apple, 2013, 63
    Apple, 2014, 4
    Cherry, 2014, 1150
    Cherry, 2013, 1180
    Fig, 2013, 467
    Fig, 2013, 374
    Fig, 2014, 162
    Fig, 2014, 267
    Fig, 2014, 586
    Orange, 2013, 10
    Orange, 2013, 50
    Orange, 2013, 62
    Orange, 2013, 131
    Orange, 2013, 145
    Orange, 2014, 93
    Orange, 2014, 102
    Pear, 2013, 27
    Pear, 2013, 157
    Pear, 2013, 384
    Pear, 2014, 489
    Pear, 2014, 782
    Plum, 2013, 148
    Plum, 2014, 36
    Plum, 2014, 412
    Plum, 2012, 700
];
```

## How to do it...

1. Drag a line chart object from the Assets panel onto the content area. Title it `Changes in Rank`.

2. Add **Year** as a dimension.

3. Add **Fruit** as a dimension.

4. Add the following expression and label it as `Sales`:

    ```
    sum({<Year={">=$(=MAX(Year)-1)<=$(=MAX(Year))"}>}Sales)
    ```

5. Under **Appearance | Colors and legend**, switch on **Show Legend** and click on Save .

6. Next, drag a bar chart onto the content area. and title it as Deviation.

7. Add **Fruit** as a dimension.

8. Add the following expression and label it as Sales Change, current year vs previous.

```
sum({<Year={$(=MAX(Year))}>}Sales)-
    sum({<Year={$(=MAX(Year)-1)}>}Sales)
```

9. Select **Horizontal** under **Appearance | Presentation**.

10. Under **Appearance | Colors and legend**, toggle the colors button to uncheck **Auto** colors and switch on custom colors. Select **By dimension** and check the **Persistent** colors button.

11. Your graphs will look similar to the following image:

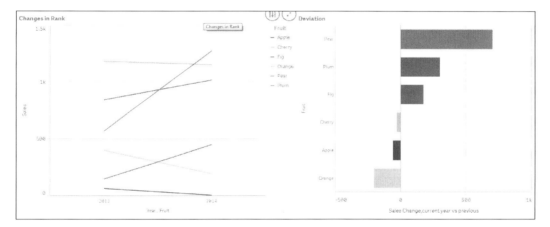

## How it works...

The first Set Analysis expression makes use of a search string; thus, defining the set of records we want to calculate across. A pseudo code will read like this.

```
Sum where the Year = {"Search for records that fulfill a
    particular requirement "}
```

Using the double quotes denotes that we will be doing a search starting with < or >. Only values that fulfill the numeric requirement will be matched.

In our example, we define the numeric requirement of the search string dynamically using the following code:

```
={">=$(=MAX(Year)-1)<=$(=MAX(Year))
```

This code evaluates the max year and the year previous to that. If we changed the -1 in the preceding code to -2 the calculation will cover three years and not just two; this is the benefit of using search strings in Set Analysis. For the second chart, we have not used a search string but specified literals. We have kept the dynamic part of the expression as:

```
{$(=MAX(Year))}
```

Now, the max year available will be picked up automatically as opposed to saying Year={2015} and updating the expression next year.

# Using comparison sets in Set Analysis

The following figure is of a stacked bar chart, a standard way of comparing separate entities. Each value that you select is displayed as a segment in each bar by year:

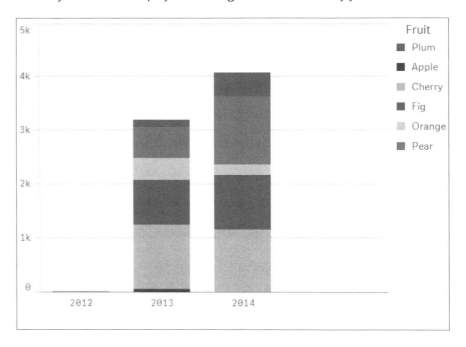

Using a comparative analysis lets you group the separate selections dynamically, so that you can compare them against each other. In the preceding example we can group together **Plum** and **Apple** versus **Fig** and **Orange**.

## Getting ready

For the purpose of this recipe, we will make use of an inline data load which gives yearly sales information for different fruits. Load the following script in the Qlik Sense data load editor:

```
Data:
LOAD * INLINE [
    Fruit, Year, Sales
    Apple, 2013, 63
    Apple, 2014, 4
    Cherry, 2014, 1150
    Cherry, 2013, 1180
    Fig, 2013, 467
    Fig, 2013, 374
    Fig, 2014, 162
    Orange, 2013, 131
    Orange, 2013, 145
    Orange, 2014, 102
    Pear, 2014, 489
    Pear, 2014, 782
    Plum, 2013, 148
    Plum, 2014, 412
];

DataIslandFruit:
LOAD * INLINE [
FruitAlt
Apple
Cherry
Fig
Orange
Pear
Plum
];
```

## How to do it...

1. Drag a bar chart onto the content area and title it `Comparison Analysis`.
2. Add **Year** as a dimension.
3. Add the following expression and label it as `Group 1 Sales`:
   ```
   Sum(Sales)
   ```

4. Add the following expression and label it as `Group 2 Sales`:

   `Sum({<Fruit={$(=GetFieldSelections(FruitAlt))}>}Sales)`

5. Under **Appearance | Colors and legend** switch on the **Show legend** option.

6. Create a Filter pane object and add the first dimension as **Fruit**. Label the dimension as `Group 1`.

7. Add **FruitAlt** as the second dimension to the Filter pane and label the dimension as `Group 2`.

8. The final chart should resemble one of the following images if you have already made the selections to test the comparative analysis.

The following is an example where no selections are made:

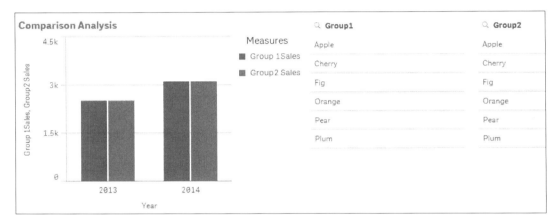

The following is an example where selections are made:

## How it works...

The second table we loaded is what's known as a data island, this table is not connected to the rest of the data model in any way. However, we can use its contents in our Set Analysis expression to compare different groups of the same field.

The first expression is completely standard. The second expression gives the total sales where the **Fruit** field (part of the complete dataset) matches the values selected in the **FruitAlt** field (part of the disconnected data island). This method allows us to select groups of data for aggregation in our graph that we can not do normally by effectively breaking the association (green, white, and grey) using Set Analysis.

# Using embedded functions in Set Analysis

As you have seen in the previous recipes, we have used functions, such as `Max()` and `GetFieldSelections()` inside our Set Analysis. Embedding the functions inside a Set Analysis expression, specifically in the rules area that defines the set of records we want to calculate across is known as dollar sign expansion.

Defining a set of records in the simplest literal form is as follows `Year= {2015}`.

The expression needs to know the year you want to use, dollar sign expansion allows us to generate the text dynamically. Understanding how to use dollar sign expansion in your Set Analysis expressions enriches the amount of analysis you can perform. Sometimes just using the function alone or specifying literals in Set Analysis is either too time consuming or adds unnecessary maintenance to the application.

## Getting ready

For the purpose of this recipe, we make use product sales data as defined in the following script. Load the following data into the Qlik Sense data editor:

```
Transactions:
Load
  date(today()-IterNo()) AS Date,
  Pick(Ceil(3*Rand()),'Standard','Premium','Discount') AS
    ProductType,
  floor(date(today()-IterNo())) AS DateNum,
  Round(1000*Rand()*Rand()*Rand()) AS Sales
Autogenerate 1000
  While Rand()<=0.9 or IterNo()=1;
```

## How to do it...

1. Create a new sheet and double click on the table object to add it to the main content area.

2. Add **Product Type** as a dimension.

3. Add the following measure as an expression, label it `Total Sales`:

   `sum(Sales)`

4. Add the following measure as the second expression, label it `WTD`:

   `sum({<DateNum={">=$(=Today()-7)"}>}Sales)`

5. Add the following measure as the third expression, label it `Previous WTD`:

   `sum({<DateNum={">=$(=Today()-14)<$(=Today()-7)"}>}Sales)`

6. Add the following as the fourth expression, label it `Weekly Variance`:

   `(COLUMN(2)-COLUMN(3))/COLUMN(2)`

7. For the expression in step 6, change the number formatting to **Number** and then select the percentage format from the drop-down list.

8. You should have a table that looks similar to the following image. The figures may not be similar to the following image as we are using the Rand function to generate the initial set of data in the script:

| ProductType | Q | Total Sales | WTD | Previous WTD | Weekly Variance |
|---|---|---|---|---|---|
| Totals | | £1,213,426 | £640,889 | £295,293 | 53.9% |
| Premium | | £410,761 | £218,494 | £97,393 | 55.4% |
| Standard | | £407,902 | £209,730 | £103,621 | 50.6% |
| Discount | | £394,763 | £212,665 | £94,279 | 55.7% |

## How it works...

When calculating something like week to date sales, the set of records you identify in your Set Analysis expression will change every day. When you use functions such as `Today()` inside the Set Analysis expression, the literal text values that the expression uses change automatically. Ultimately using dollar sign expansion is just a replacement for the text strings that you could use.

If the date today is `06/08/2015` then. The user see the set condition as:

`DateNum={">=$(=Today()-7)"}`

While Qlik Sense sees the set condition as:

```
DateNum={">=31/07/2015"}
```

This is because the function inside the dollar sign is evaluated first and it simply expands into the text/field values that we want to calculate across.

## There's more...

The fourth expression is written as:

`(COLUMN(2)-COLUMN(3))/COLUMN(2)`. Here we pick up the column numbers instead of the actual field names for our calculation.

We can also write the expression in the following manner:

`([WTD]-[Previous WTD])/[WTD]` .

We will get a bad field name: `([WTD]-[Previous WTD])/[WTD]` at the bottom of the Expression editor window. But don't worry, as Qlik Sense will still interpret the results correctly. This chink may be ironed out in future releases of Qlik Sense.

The expression does not make use of the fields that we have loaded into the applications data model. It instead uses the expression labels we have already created for the previous calculations. This is always a best practice option if you need to use the same calculation in the same table more than once. It make things simpler, you only have to change something once and best of all it is optimized and the calculation is already cached in RAM.

# Creating a multi-measure expression in Set Analysis

Sometimes you may have groups of expressions you want to view that either they don't need to be viewed at once or you don't have the room to display them all. In these cases you do not have to go and create another sheet, you can add a control to let users select what is calculated.

The output of this recipe is similar to the preceding recipe, only with slightly different expressions to add depth of analysis in the same object.

## Getting ready

For the purpose of this recipe, we make use product sales and margin data as defined in the following script. Load the following data into the data editor:

```
Transactions:
Load
Date(today()-IterNo()) AS Date,
Pick(Ceil(3*Rand()),'Standard','Premium','Discount') AS
  ProductType,
Floor(date(today()-IterNo())) AS DateNum,
 Round(1000*Rand()*Rand()*Rand()) AS Sales,
 Round(10*Rand()*Rand()*Rand()) AS Quantity,
 Round(Rand()*Rand(),0.00001) AS Margin
Autogenerate 10000
While Rand()<=0.9 or IterNo()=1;

Measures:
LOAD * INLINE [
    Measures
    Sales
    Quantity
    Margin
];
```

## How to do it...

1.  Create a Filter pane object and add **Measures** as the dimension.

2.  Next, drag across a table object onto the main content area.

3.  Add **Product Type** as a dimension

4.  Add the following expression as the first measure and label it `Total Sales`:

    ```
    sum($(=GetFieldSelections(Measures)))
    ```

5.  Add the following expression as the second measure and label it `WTD`:

    ```
    sum({<DateNum={">=$(=Today()-
       7)"}>}$(=GetFieldSelections(Measures)))
    ```

6.  Add the following measure as the third expression and label it `Previous WTD`:

    ```
    sum({<DateNum={">=$(=Today()-14)<$(=Today()-7)"}>}
       $(=GetFieldSelections(Measures)))
    ```

7.  Add the following as the fourth expression and label it `Weekly Variance`:

    ```
    (COLUMN(2)-COLUMN(3))/COLUMN(2)
    ```

8. For the expression in step 7 change the number formatting to **Number** and then select the percentage format from the drop-down list.

9. If you come out of the Edit mode and select one value from the Filter pane object, you can see the calculation changing.

10. You should have a table that looks similar to the following image. The figures may not be exactly similar to the following image since we are using the Rand function to generate the initial set of data in the script:

| Select one option below to view the figures | | | | | |
|---|---|---|---|---|---|
| Chart Options | ProductType | Total | WTD | Previous WTD | Weekly Variance |
| Sales ✓ | Totals | £12,739,229 | 6,609,537 | £3,243,454 | 50.9% |
| Margin | Discount | £4,278,988 | 2,218,842 | £1,088,209 | 51.0% |
| Quantity | Premium | £4,237,879 | 2,203,479 | £1,080,869 | 50.9% |
| | Standard | £4,222,362 | 2,187,216 | £1,074,376 | 50.9% |

## How it works...

Here we capture the field values that we want to calculate using a data island. When we use a data island, we simply pick an option from the measures box without filtering the data in any way. But this approach allows us to control what calculations are being returned.

The `GetFieldSelections (Measures)` function simply returns **Sales**, **Margin**, or **Quantity** depending on what you have selected. As such, writing the expression `Sum (GetFieldSelections (Measures))` means we can have any of the three options displayed just by selecting the value from the Filter pane.

As mentioned in the previous recipe, we can write the `Weekly Variance` expression using the expression labels previously defined in the table as follows:

```
([WTD]-[Previous WTD])/[WTD]
```

We will get a warning for "Bad field" at the bottom of the Expression editor window. Ignore it, as this chink may be ironed out in future releases of Qlik Sense.

# Using search strings inside a set modifier

A set modifier contains one or several field names that make up the set expression. We can define a *range of values* within the selection made in the set modifier. The following recipe makes use of search strings to calculate the sales for customers within a specified date range.

## Getting ready

For the purpose of this recipe, we will be using an inline data load which contain shipment details for each customer. Load the following script within the Qlik Sense data load editor:

```
Sales:
LOAD DATE(Date#(DeliveryDate,'DD/MM/YYYY')) AS DeliveryDate,
DATE(Date#(ShipmentDate,'DD/MM/YYYY')) AS ShipmentDate,
Customer,Month,Volume,Sales,Supplier INLINE [
Customer,Month,DeliveryDate,ShipmentDate,Volume,Sales,Supplier
ABC,Jan,01/01/2015,29/12/2014,100,10000,DEF
ABC,Feb,02/02/2015,25/01/2015,100,10000,DEF
ABC,Mar,03/03/2015,02/03/2015,400,12000,DEF
ABC,Apr,04/04/2015,24/01/2015,100,10000,GHI
DEF,Feb,03/02/2015,03/02/2015,200,25000,GHI
DEF,Mar,25/03/2015,21/03/2015,300,25000,GHI
DEF,Apr,18/04/2015,14/04/2015,200,25000,ABC
GHI,Jan,24/01/2015,18/01/2015,200,8500,ABC
GHI,Mar,14/03/2015,09/03/2015,200,7000,ABC
GHI,Jun,11/06/2015,07/06/2015,200,5000,ABC
];
```

## How to do it...

1. Drag across the Table object from the Assets panel on to the sheet.

2. Add **Customer** as dimension.

3. Add the following measure, which calculates the sales for delivery dates ranging between `14/01/2015` and `14/04/2015`. Label the measure as `Sales`:

```
Sum({< DeliveryDate = {'>=$(=DATE(Date#('14/01/2015',
   'DD/MM/YYYY')))<=$(=DATE(Date#('14/04/2015',
   'DD/MM/YYYY')))'} >} Sales)
```

4. Click on **Save** and .

5. The resultant table will be as following. Note that we get a subset of the `Sales` value based on the date range specified in the set modifier:

| Sales | |
|---|---|
| Customer | Sales |
| **Totals** | **97500** |
| ABC | 32000 |
| DEF | 50000 |
| GHI | 15500 |

6. Drag across the Filter pane object onto the sheet and add the **DeliveryDate** as dimension.

7. Select any random delivery dates. Observe that the **Sales** figure for each customer remains unchanged.

## How it works...

In the set modifier we specify two dates enclosed within single quotes (`' '`). The first date is the start date of the range and it is preceded by a `>=` sign, while the second date is an end date of the range and is preceded by a `<=` sign. We use a date function in order to interpret the strings as date. The `$` sign expansion evaluates the expression inside the bracket.

## There's more...

The preceding recipe considers two static dates for the date range. We can also make the date range dynamic by tweaking our Set Analysis expression the following way:

```
Sum({<DeliveryDate =
    {">=$(=min(ShipmentDate))<=$(=max(ShipmentDate))"} >} Sales )
```

Here we are comparing the delivery date to the shipment date and calculating sales for the delivery dates lying between the range of shipment dates.

For example:

1. Add **ShipmentDate** as a new dimension in the Filter pane object.

2. Select the shipment dates from **18/01/2015** to **25/01/2015**.

3. The resultant table shows the sales value only for the delivery date, as **24/01/2015**:

## See also

▶ Using the = sign with variables in Set Analysis

# Capturing a list of field values using a concat() function in Set Analysis

While we have used the search strings in previous recipes to do numeric search, we can also do text searches by using the wild card character *. However, sometimes you might want to compare the values in one field to the values stored in another. We can also achieve this using Set Analysis and the concat() function.

## Getting ready

For the purpose of this recipe, we make use product sales data as defined in the following script. Load the following script into the data load editor:

```
Transactions:
Load *,
    If(Len(TmpSubCategory)=0,Null(),TmpSubCategory) AS
    SubCategory;
Load * INLINE [
    ProductType, Category, TmpSubCategory, Sales
    Premium,A4,A4,300
    Standard,A4,A4,100
    Premium,A5,A5,500
    Standard,A5,A5,200
    Premium,A6,A6,1000
    Standard,A6,A6,600
    Premium,A1,,700
    Standard,A1,,300
    Premium,A2,,300
    Premium,A3,,200
    Standard,A3,,60
];
```

## How to do it...

1. Drag a table object onto the content area and label it as `Product Sales`.
2. Add **Product Type** as a dimension
3. Add the following expression as the first measure and label it as `Total Sales`:

   `Sum (Sales)`

4. Add the following expression as the second measure and label it as `Sub Category Sales`:

   `Sum ({<Category = {$(=concat (distinct [SubCategory], ','))} >} Sales)`

5. You should have a table that looks similar to the following image:

| Product Sales | | |
|---|---|---|
| ProductType 🔍 | Total Sales | Sub category Sales |
| Totals | 4260 | 2700 |
| Premium | 3000 | 1800 |
| Standard | 1260 | 900 |

## How it works...

The `concat ()` function wraps around a field name; when expressed it lists every field value separated by a delimiter. As such, the function `concat (Distinct Subcategory,',')` returns A4, A5, A6, which are all the values in the sub-category field with no selections made.

Using the `concat ()` function means you can avoid having to write out large lists of text strings in your Set Analysis expression. Even better, if these lists come from a source system where they are automatically updated with data.

# Using the element functions P() and E() in Set Analysis

So far we have seen how the sets can be used to manipulate the result of an expression. To take the concept a bit further, we will now see how to use the `P ()` and `E ()` functions inside a Set Analysis expression. In the previous Set Analysis expressions, all field values were explicitly defined in the sets or variables or in certain cases through defined searches. The `P ()` and `E ()` functions make use of nested set definitions.

A P() function returns a set of all possible values while an E() function returns a set of all excluded values.

## Getting ready

For the purpose of this recipe, we make use customer sales data as defined in the following inline data load. Load the following script in Qlik Sense data load editor:

```
P_E:
LOAD * INLINE [
Customer,Month,Volume,Sales,Supplier
ABC,Jan,100,10000,DEF
ABC,Feb,100,10000,DEF
ABC,Mar,400,12000,DEF
ABC,Apr,100,10000,GHI
DEF,Feb,200,25000,GHI
DEF,Mar,300,25000,GHI
DEF,Apr,200,25000,ABC
GHI,Jan,200,8500,ABC
GHI,Mar,200,7000,ABC
GHI,Jun,200,5000,ABC
];
```

## How to do it...

1. On a new sheet, drag and drop the table object from the Assets panel on the left-hand side of the screen. Name the table as Possible Sales.

2. Add **Customer** and **Month** as dimensions.

3. Add the following expression for Sales:

   Sum({$<Customer=P({1<Month={'Jan'}>})>}Sales)

4. Click on **Save** and [✎ Done].

5. The resultant table will look similar to the following. Note that it only shows all the records for customers **ABC** and **GHI**:

**Possible Sales**

| Customer | Month | Sales |
|---|---|---|
| Totals | | 62500 |
| ABC | Mar | 12000 |
| ABC | Apr | 10000 |
| ABC | Feb | 10000 |
| ABC | Jan | 10000 |
| GHI | Jan | 8500 |
| GHI | Mar | 7000 |
| GHI | Jun | 5000 |

6. Next, create another table with the same dimensions, such as **Customer** and **Month** and name it `Excluded Sales`.

7. Add the `Sales` expression as follows:

```
Sum({$<Customer=E({1<Month={'Jan'}>})>}Sales)
```

8. The resultant table will look similar to the following screen shot. Note that we only have one customer **DEF** in the table:

**Excluded Sales**

| Customer | Month | Sales |
|---|---|---|
| Totals | | 75000 |
| DEF | Apr | 25000 |
| DEF | Feb | 25000 |
| DEF | Mar | 25000 |

## How it works...

1. The `P()` function selects all the possible values from the set. In the first expression:

```
Sum({$<Customer=P({1<Month={'Jan'}>})>}Sales)
```

We select the customers who have made sales in the month of January.

2. However, the `E()` function selects all the excluded values from the set. In the second expression:

```
Sum({$<Customer=E({1<Month={'Jan'}>})>}Sales)
```

We select the customers who have made sales in all months except January.

## There's more...

The concept of `P()` and `E()` can also be used with two fields for comparison inside the nested sets.

For example: if one needs to find out all those customers where the suppliers had a volume of `300`, the set expression will be defined in the following way:

```
Sum({$<Customer=p({1<Volume={300}>}Supplier)>}Sales)
```

Here, the element function `P()` returns a list of possible suppliers who had a volume of `300`. The list of suppliers is then matched to the customers to make the relevant selections.

The resultant table will look similar to the following:

| Possible Sales | | | |
|---|---|---|---|
| Customer 🔍 | Month 🔍 | Volume 🔍 | Sales |
| **Totals** | | | **20500** |
| GHI | Jan | 200 | 8500 |
| GHI | Mar | 200 | 7000 |
| GHI | Jun | 200 | 5000 |

An `E()` function in place of `P()` will result in all the customers whose suppliers never had a volume of `300`:

| Excluded Sales | | |
|---|---|---|
| Customer 🔍 | Month 🔍 | Sales |
| **Totals** | | **117000** |
| ABC | Mar | 12000 |
| ABC | Apr | 10000 |
| ABC | Feb | 10000 |
| ABC | Jan | 10000 |
| DEF | Apr | 25000 |
| DEF | Feb | 25000 |
| DEF | Mar | 25000 |

## See also

▶  *Using embedded functions in Set Analysis*

# 7

# Extensions in Qlik Sense®

In this chapter, we will focus on some of the advanced visualization techniques in Qlik Sense and discuss the following topics:

- ► Creating an HTML visualization extension for Qlik Sense®
- ► Defining a Properties panel in Qlik Sense® visualizations
- ► Creating custom components within Qlik Sense® visualizations
- ► Using data with extensions

## Introduction

Before we jump the gun, it is expected of the user to have an intermediate level of JavaScript and HTML knowledge to develop extensions in Qlik Sense.

Qlik Sense has an extensive library of chart objects to display data. However, of late there has been an increase in the demand for custom visualizations from business users and such visualizations are used in specific circumstances. Similar to Qlikview, we can also develop visualization extension objects in Qlik Sense using open standards, such as HTML5, CSS, and JavaScript.

However, the method to create these extensions differs in Qlik Sense. Qlik Sense visualizations are compatible with an AJAX interface or any other web browser. We can also use JavaScript code from external visual libraries, such as D3 to make intuitive and user friendly extension objects.

The following recipes discuss different concepts in advanced visualizations, such as HTML extensions, custom components, and use of data with extensions.

# Creating an HTML visualization extension for Qlik Sense®

To begin with, let us discuss a recipe to create a simple HTML extension in Qlik Sense. The two files that are mandatory to create any Qlik Sense extension are:

- `.JS` file: This file contains the JavaScript required to implement the extension and is built around the RequireJS framework
- `.QEXT` file: This is an extension metadata file, which contains the JSON description to be used within the desktop client

In addition to the preceding mandatory files, one can also make use of additional files, such as:

- Script files from external libraries such as D3 or Raphael
- CSS files: To add styles to the extensions
- Images, Fonts, Icons, and so on

The default directory for Qlik Sense Desktop extensions is `C:\Users\[UserName]\ Documents\Qlik\Sense\Extensions\`.

In this example we will print the words "Hello World" on the screen using our first Qlik Sense extension. This is a common first task used when we learn various programming languages. The idea is to keep the code as simple as possible while providing information on the structure of the code and anatomy of the extension environment.

 A little slice of history: Using the "Hello, World" example dates back as far 1974. The first known version in computer literature was taken from a 1974 Bell Laboratories internal memorandum on programming in C.

## Getting ready

This recipe is built entirely from the *How to do it...* section and does not require data to be loaded first. We use notepad to write the code in the following examples. A suggested alternative is Notepad++, which the user can download separately. Notepad++ is a free tool that improves the readability of the code by highlighting methods, functions, and so on.

Taking into consideration the two mandatory files, let's start creating a simple extension using HTML:

1. Create a folder called as `QlikSense Cookbook – Hello World` to store the `.JS` and `.QEXT` files.

2. The folder should be created under `C:\Users\[UserName]\Documents\Qlik\Sense\Extensions\`.

## How to do it...

1. In the `QlikSense Cookbook – Hello World` folder, create a new notepad document and add the following code:

```
{
    "name" : " QlikSense Cookbook - Hello World",
    "description" : "QlikSense Cookbook - Chapter 7, Recipe
    1: Hello World.",
    "icon" : "extension",
        "type" : "visualization",
        "version": "1",
    "preview" : "bar",
    "author": "Your Name"
}
```

2. Click on **Save As** in the notepad document and change the **Save as type** to **All Files (\*.\*)**.

3. Call the file name `QlikSense-Cookbook-C7-R1-HelloWorld.qext`.

4. Create another blank notepad file in the same location and add the following code:

```
define( [
        'jquery'
    ],
    function ( $ ) {
        'use strict';
        return {
      paint:function ( $element, layout ) {
      $element.empty();
                var $helloWorld  = $(
                document.createElement( 'div' ) );
                $helloWorld.html('Hello World from the
                extension "QlikSense Cookbook -
                HelloWorld"<br/>');
                $element.append( $helloWorld);
            }
        };
    } );
```

5.  Click on **Save As** in the notepad document and change the **Save as type** to **All Files (*.*)**. Call the file named `QlikSense-Cookbook-C7-R1-HelloWorld.js`.

6.  Create a new application in Qlik Sense Desktop and name it `QlikSenseCookBook_ Extensions`.

7.  Open the data load editor and load the following code:

    ```
    LOAD 1 as Dummy AUTOGENERATE(1);
    ```

8.  Once the script is successfully run, open the **App overview** from the Navigation dropdown at the top. Create a new sheet and go to the Edit mode.

9.  In the visualization area, we will be able to see the extension alongside the normal default visualizations with the name **QlikSense Cookbook-Hello world**.

10. Drag across the object onto the sheet.

11. Add the **Title** as `Qlik Sense Extension`.

12. The resultant object on the screen should look similar to the following:

> **Qlik Sense Extension**
>
> Hello World from the extension "QlikSense Cookbook - HelloWorld"

## How it works...

The `QlikSense-Cookbook-C7-R1-HelloWorld.js` contains the JavaScript to build what the extension will actually do. It is formed of two main parts **Define** and **Paint**:

▶ **Define**: This is used to define the dependencies in the JavaScript file. It follows the concept specified in the RequireJS framework. In our recipe we have not loaded any external dependency. However, if the need arises, this can be loaded prior to the execution of the main script.

▶ **Paint**: This is the main part of the script which basically renders the visualization. It is formed of two parts `$element` and `layout`:

  ❏ `$element` contains the HTML content

  ❏ `layout` contains the data and properties of the extension

The `QlikSense-Cookbook-C7-R1-HelloWorld.qext` file contains the metadata about the extension, such as the name, description, icon, type, version, and author. Out of these, the `name` and `type` properties are mandatory.

The basic structure of a `.qext` file is shown in the following code:

```
{
    "name" : "QlikSense Cookbook - Hello World",
    "description" : " QlikSense Cookbook, Simple Hello World.",
    "preview" : "bar",
    "icon" : "extension",
    "type" : "visualization",
    "version": "1",
    "author": "Your Name"
}
```

The first four lines control what is displayed in the following image:

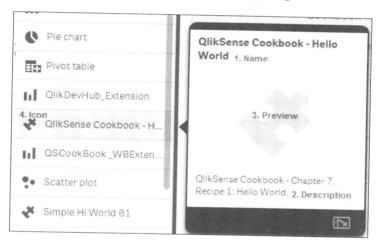

The type should always be "visualization". The default value for an icon is "extension" but it can be changed to a predefined list of icon names, such as the "Line chart", "Bar chart", and so on. This specifies the icon displayed in the Assets panel besides the extension object:

- ▸ **version**: Specifies the version of the extension
- ▸ **author**: Specifies the author of the extension

One can also define a preview image for the extension object under the `preview` property in the `.qext` file. For example "Preview": `QSExtension.png`. The `.PNG` file must be stored in the same folder as the extension.

If we don't define the preview image, then the Icon definition will supersede.

## There's more...

The extension discussed in the preceding recipe displays static text **Hello World** from the extension of "QlikSense Cookbook - HelloWorld". However, we can make it dynamic by making some simple additions to the code, as discussed in the following steps:

1. Open the `QlikSense-Cookbook-C7-R1-HelloWorld.js` file.

2. Inside `Define` add another object called `definition` which describes the basic design of the property panel for the extension object:

```
definition: {
    type: "items",
    component: "accordion",
    items: {
        appearancePanel: {
            uses: "settings",
            items: {
                QSPropertyPanel: {
                    ref: "QSDynamicExtension",
                    type: "string",
                    label: "QlikSense extension Text"
                }
            }
        }
    }
},
```

3. In order to render what we enter in the text box defined in step 1, we need to enter the `console.log(layout);` statement at the start of the paint block.

4. Finally, to make the result dynamic, modify the output statement to:

```
'$helloWorld   .html(layout. QSDynamicExtension);'
```

5. The final code in the `QlikSense-Cookbook-C7-R1-HelloWorld.js` file should look like the following code:

```
define( [
        'jquery'
    ],
    function ( $ ) {
        'use strict';
        return {
    definition: {
     type: "items",
     component: "accordion",
     items: {
         appearancePanel: {
             uses: "settings",
             items: {
                 QSPropertyPanel: {
```

```
                ref: "QSDynamicExtension",
                type: "string",
                label: "QlikSense extension Text"
            }
        }
    }
    }
},
            paint: function ( $element, layout ) {
    console.log(layout);
    $element.empty();
            var $helloWorld  =
            $(document.createElement('div'));
              $helloWorld.html(layout.QSDynamicExtension);
              $element.append($helloWorld);
        }
    };
    }
);
```

6. Refresh your Qlik Sense document by pressing *F5* before implementing the new dynamic extension.

7. The Properties panel of the resultant extension object will look like the following image:

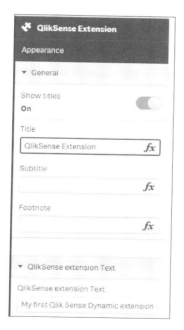

8. Put any desired text in the **QlikSense extension Text** box and check results.

## See also

Creating a Qlik Sense® visualization using Qlik Dev Hub in *Chapter 7, Extensions in Qlik Sense*®.

# Defining a Properties panel in Qlik Sense® visualizations

Typically, the most common properties used by any Qlik Sense visualization are Dimensions, Measures, and Appearance. The appearance section is included by default when we create any Qlik Sense visualization, even if the Properties panel is not defined.

We can extend the definition of these properties in the JavaScript code to reuse the built in sections. The following recipe demonstrates how to define and extend the definitions of properties in Qlik Sense visualization and further reference these properties in our code.

## Getting ready

This recipe is a continuation of the previous recipe. So, we will be using the same `QlikSense-Cookbook-C7-R1-HelloWorld.js` file, which contains the code for the dynamic extension as discussed in the *There's more...* section.

## How to do it...

1. Open the `QlikSense-Cookbook-C7-R1-HelloWorld.js` file located at `C:\ Users\<username>\Documents\Qlik\Sense\Extensions\ QlikSense Cookbook – Hello World\`.

2. We have reused the settings section while creating the dynamic extension, which is nothing but the internal name for the **Appearance** section.

3. Next, we will extend the definition to reuse other built-in sections. In this example we will reuse the sorting sections.

4. Add the following piece of code after the `QSpropertyPanel` under `items`:

```
sorting: {
    uses: "sorting"
}
```

5. Save the JavaScript file and refresh your Qlik Sense application at this stage so that the "QlikSense Cookbook – Hello World" gets updated. The Properties panel for the extension will look similar to the following image:

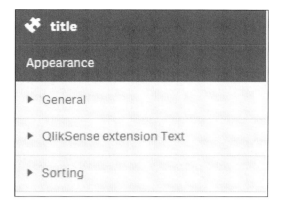

6. We will output some values to the paint method by inserting the code as shown in the following code inside the `paint` function:

```
console.info('paint >> layout >> ', layout);
$element.empty();
        var $helloWorld   =
        $(document.createElement('div'));
          // Variable holding the output
          var html = '<b>Property values:</b><br/>';
          html += 'Title: ' + layout.title + '<br/>';
          html += 'SubTitle: ' + layout.subtitle +
          '<br/>';
      // Assigning the variable to our output
      container
  $helloWorld.html( html );
//$helloWorld.html(layout.QSDynamicExtension);
        $element.append($helloWorld);
```

7. The final script for the `QlikSense-Cookbook-C7-R1-HelloWorld.js` file will look like the following code:

```
define ( [
        'jquery'
    ],
    function ( $ ) {
        'use strict';
        return {
    definition: {
     type: "items",
     component: "accordion",
     items: {
```

```
            appearancePanel: {
                uses: "settings",
                items: {
                    QSPropertyPanel: {
                        ref: "QSDynamicExtension",
                        type: "string",
                        label: "QlikSense extension Text"
                    },

            sorting: {
                uses: "sorting"
            }

                }
            }
        }
    },
            paint: function ( $element, layout ) {
  //console.log(layout);
   console.info('paint >> layout >> ', layout);
  $element.empty();
                var $helloWorld   =
                $(document.createElement('div'));
  // Variable holding the output
  var html = '<b>Property values:</b><br/>';
  html += 'Title: ' + layout.title + '<br/>';
  html += 'SubTitle: ' + layout.subtitle + '<br/>';
                // Assigning the variable to our output
                //container
    $helloWorld.html( html );
                $element.append($helloWorld);
            }
        };
    }
);
```

8.  The changes we made in the JavaScript file will introduce the, **Property Values,** section to the Properties panel.

9.  Save the file and return back to the Qlik Sense application.

10. Create a new sheet.

11. Go to the [ ✎ **Edit** ] mode.

12. On the left hand side pane, you will notice the extension object "QlikSense Cookbook –Hello World". Drag the extension object onto the sheet.

13. Next, go to the General section under Properties and add **Title** as `Qlik Sense`
    `CookBook-Hello World` and **SubTitle** as `Chapter 7`.

14. The resulting output will be as follows:

> **Qlik Sense CookBook-HelloWorld**
>
> Chapter 7
>
> **Property values:**
> Title: Qlik Sense CookBook-HelloWorld
> SubTitle: Chapter 7

## How it works...

We reference the defined properties in our JavaScript file under the `paint` section. We use
a `layout` parameter that includes the current scope of the visualization extension together
with the properties; `this` parameter is passed to the `paint` method.

## There's more...

We can use other native Qlik Sense properties in our Properties panel definitions such as
Dimension, Measure, Data Handling, Reference lines, and so on. For more information on the
Add-Ons go to the following address:

```
https://help.qlik.com/sense/2.0/en-US/developer/#../Subsystems/
Extensions/Content/extensions-reusing-properties.htm%3FTocPath%3D
Building%2520visualization%2520extensions%7CGetting%2520started%
2520building%2520visualization%2520extensions%7CBuilding%2520a%25-
20properties%2520panel%7C_____1
```

# Creating custom components within Qlik Sense® visualizations

Other than the predefined properties, the user may want to create custom components to
alter the properties of the extension object. This is done in the appearance according to the
main JavaScript file. The use of custom components provides the user with more options to
customize the extension objects from the Properties panel.

The list of different UI components that you can use in the custom properties is as follows:

- Check box
- Input box/Text box
- Drop down list

- ▸ Radio button
- ▸ Button group
- ▸ Switch
- ▸ Slider
- ▸ Range-slider

## Getting ready

This recipe is a continuation from the previous recipe. So we will be using the `QlikSense-Cookbook-C7-R1-HelloWorld.js` file for this recipe as well, which we created for dynamic extensions in the *There's more...* section.

The recipe explains the procedure to create a check box in the Properties panel.

## How to do it...

1. Open the `QlikSense-Cookbook-C7-R1-HelloWorld.js` file located at `C:\ Users\<username>\Documents\Qlik\Sense\Extensions\ QlikSense Cookbook - Hello World\`.

2. Next, we will add the property definition of the custom Check box as a new accordion item. This will be put inside the return block under items.

3. The definition of check box will be as follows:

```
MyAccordion: {
        type: "boolean",
        label: "Show me",
        ref: "myproperties.show",
        defaultValue: true
        },
```

4. The final script for the `QlikSense-Cookbook-C7-R1-HelloWorld.js` file will look like the following code:

```
define( [
        'jquery'
    ],
    function ( $ ) {
        'use strict';
        return {
    definition: {
     type: "items",
     component: "accordion",
     items: {
            MyAccordion: {
```

```
            type: "boolean",
            label: "Show me",
            ref: "myproperties.show",
            defaultValue: true
        },

        appearancePanel: {
            uses: "settings",
            items: {
                QSPropertyPanel: {
                    ref: "QSDynamicExtension",
                    type: "string",
                    label: "QlikSense extension Text"
                }
            }
        }
    }
},
        paint: function ( $element, layout ) {
console.log(layout);
$element.empty();
            var $helloWorld  =
            $(document.createElement('div'));
             $helloWorld.html(layout.QSDynamicExtension);
             $element.append($helloWorld);
        }
    };
    }
);
```

5.   Save the file and return back to the Qlik Sense application.

6.   Create a new sheet.

7.   Go to the [✎ **Edit**] mode.

8.   On the left-hand side pane, you will find the extension object "QlikSense CookBook – Hello World". Drag the extension object onto the sheet.

9.   The Properties panel to the right displays the **Show me** checkbox as the following image:

## How it works...

The definition for each of the custom properties is stated in the definition block of the code in the main JavaScript file of the extension.

In our example, the definition for the check box contains four fields namely `type`, `ref`, `label`, and `defaultvalue`. The field `type` is mandatory and should be assigned a `Boolean` value for a check box property definition.

- `label` is used to label the check box with a header in the Properties panel
- `ref` is an Id to refer to the check box property
- `defaultvalue` defines the default value for the check box

## There's more...

In a way similar to the one described in the preceding recipe, you can also define properties to create sliders, radio buttons, description boxes, and so on. The following URL reflects upon the procedure to create all these custom components:

```
https://help.qlik.com/sense/2.0/en-US/developer/#../Subsystems/
Extensions/Content/Howtos/working-with-custom-properties.htm
```

# Using data with extensions

In the previous recipes in this chapter we created our first Hello World extension, added properties and added custom components to the properties. Now, it's time to get your hands on the data inside your application.

We will go a step further in this recipe and define "Dimensions" and "Measures" in our JavaScript code block. This way we can extract the data from the tables and display it in a chart on our Qlik Sense sheet.

## Getting ready

1. Open Qlik Sense hub and create a new Qlik Sense application.
2. Load the following script in order to auto-generate some example data:

```
Transactions:
Load *,
 mod(TransID,26)+1 AS Period,
 Pick(Ceil(3*Rand1),'Standard','Premium','Discount') AS
  ProductType,
```

```
Pick(Ceil(6*Rand1),'Apple','Orange','Cherry','Plum',
  'Fig','Pear') AS Category,
Round(1000*Rand()*Rand()*Rand1) AS Sales,
Round(Rand()*Rand1,0.00001) AS Margin;
Load
  date(41275+IterNo()-1) AS Date,
  Rand() AS Rand1,
  RecNo() AS TransID
Autogenerate 1000 While Rand()<=0.5 or IterNo()=1;
```

3. Save the application.

## How to do it...

1. Create a new folder in the extension directory and call it `Qlik Sense Cookbook-C7-R3 - Hello Data`.

2. Create a new `.qext` file, as we did in the first recipe of this chapter and name it `Qlik Sense Cookbook-C7-R3 - Hello Data.qext`. In the `.qext` file use the following code:

```
{
    "name" : "Hello Data",
    "description" : "Examples how to use data in
    visualization extensions.",
    "icon" : "extension",
    "type" : "visualization",
    "version": "0.1.0",
    "author": "Your Name"
}
```

3. Next, create the JavaScript (`.js`) file, as we did previously in the same folder location and name it `Qlik Sense Cookbook-C7-R3 - Hello Data.js`. Enter the following code:

```
define( [],
    function ( ) {
        'use strict';
        return {
            definition: {
                type: "items",
                component: "accordion",
                items: {
                    dimensions: {uses: "dimensions"},
                    measures: {uses: "measures"},
                    sorting: {uses: "sorting"},
                    appearance: {uses: "settings"}
```

```
                    }
                },
                initialProperties: {
                    qHyperCubeDef: {
                        qDimensions: [],
                        qMeasures: [],
                        qInitialDataFetch: [
                            {
                                qWidth: 10,
                                qHeight: 100
                            }
                        ]
                    }
                },
                paint: function ( $element, layout ) {
                    var hc = layout.qHyperCube;
                    //console.log( 'Data returned: ', hc );
                    // Default rendering with HTML injection
                    $element.empty();
                    var table = '<table border="1">';
table += '<thead>';
table += '<tr>';
for (var i = 0; i < hc.qDimensionInfo.length; i++) {
table += '<th>' + hc.qDimensionInfo[i].qFallbackTitle +
  '</th>';}
 for (var i = 0; i < hc.qMeasureInfo.length; i++) {
table += '<th>' + hc.qMeasureInfo[i].qFallbackTitle +
  '</th>';}
                    table += '</tr>';
            table += '</thead>';
                    table += '<tbody>';
for (var r = 0; r < hc.qDataPages[0].qMatrix.length; r++) {
            table += '<tr>';
for (var c = 0; c < hc.qDataPages[0].qMatrix[r].length;
  c++) {
            table += '<td>';
            table += hc.qDataPages[0].qMatrix[r][c].qText;
            table += '</td>';
                            }
```

```
                              table += '</tr>';
                      }
                  table += '</tbody>';
              table += '</table>';
              $element.append( table );
          }
      };
  } );
```

4. Go to the **App overview** and create a new sheet in Qlik Sense.

5. Go to the [ ✎ **Edit** ] mode.

6. From the left-hand side Assets panel, drag across the "Hello Data" extension, which we created just now.

7. Title the **Object** as Margin Analysis.

8. Add **Category** as a dimension.

9. Add the following measure and label it as Margin:

   Sum(Margin)

10. The final result will be similar to the following image:

**Margin Analysis**

| Category | Margin |
| --- | --- |
| Apple | 15.37643 |
| Cherry | 71.21623 |
| Fig | 115.43042 |
| Orange | 41.11345 |
| Pear | 144.92144 |
| Plum | 101.98290 |

11. The resultant table will look like the following image. Also observe that while in the Edit mode for the object, the property panel to the right shows properties, such as **Dimensions**, **Measures**, **Sorting**, and **Appearance;** similar to a normal Qlik Sense object.

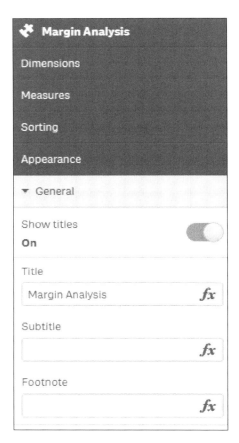

## How it works...

In the previous recipes, we have already looked at the code to define the properties pane. This section of the code allows us to reuse the built in capability to define dimensions and measures just like the other objects in Qlik Sense:

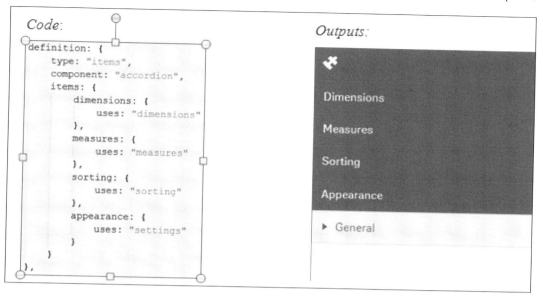

By setting the default items in the properties window to include standard dimensions and measures options, we can now add data to the visualization. The data fields can be added directly in the object as shown in the following image:

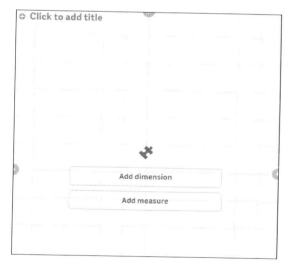

As soon as you add dimensions and measures to a visualization extension, the Qlik Engine will return what is known as a **HyperCube**. Although it is a huge simplification, you can simply think of it as a table returned from the engine.

For a full breakdown of the HyperCube structure, see the QlikSense development toolkit on `qlik.com`. For now, we are interested in three objects of the HyperCube and they are:

- `layout.qHyperCube.qDimensionInfo`: used dimensions
- `layout.qHyperCube.qMeasureInfo`: used measures
- `layout.qHyperCube.qDataPages`: the result

In the `print` statement, we create a basic HTML table with a header for labels and body for the data. The skeleton of a basic HTML table is shown in the following code:

```
var table = '<table border="1">';
  table += '<thead>';
  table += '</thead>';

  table += '<tbody>';
  table += '</tbody>';
table += '</table>';
```

The first two bullet points in the preceding section are used for `qDimensionInfo` and `qMeasureInfo`. The third bullet point is for `qDataPages`:

- `qDataPages` is an array
- The data is held with `qDataPages[0].qDataPages.qMatrix`
- It is also an array of objects (the rows)
- Each holds an array of other objects (the cells)

The preceding skeleton has been completed in our example and is shown in the following image:

The following image is the result of the header:

```
table += '<thead>';
    table += '<tr>';
    for (var i = 0; i < hc.qDimensionInfo.length; i++) {
        table += '<th>' + hc.qDimensionInfo[i].qFallbackTitle + '</th>';
    }
    for (var i = 0; i < hc.qMeasureInfo.length; i++) {
        table += '<th>' + hc.qMeasureInfo[i].qFallbackTitle + '</th>';
    }
table += '</tr>';
table += '</thead>';
```

The following image is the result of the body:

```
table += '<tbody>';
    for (var r = 0; r < hc.qDataPages[0].qMatrix.length; r++) {
        table += '<tr>';
        for (var c = 0; c < hc.qDataPages[0].qMatrix[r].length; c++) {
            table += '<td>';
                table += hc.qDataPages[0].qMatrix[r][c].qText;
            table += '</td>';
        }
        table += '</tr>';
    }
table += '</tbody>';
```

## See also

▸  *Creating an HTML visualization extension for Qlik Sense®*

# 8
# What's New in Version 2.1.1?

In this chapter, we will focus on some of the latest features that have been released in Qlik Sense Version 2.1.1:

▶ Using the visual exploration capability in Qlik Sense®

▶ Defining Variables in Qlik Sense®

▶ Exporting stories to MS PowerPoint

▶ Using the Qlik Dev Hub in Qlik Sense® 2.1.1

▶ Using Extension editor in Qlik Dev Hub

▶ Using Qlik Dev Hub to generate mashups

▶ Embedding Qlik Sense® application on a website using a single configurator

▶ Using the Qlik DataMarket

▶ Using Smart Search

▶ Creating dynamic charts in Qlik Sense®

▶ Using smart data load profiling

## Introduction

This chapter deals with some new functionalities introduced in the latest release of Qlik Sense 2.1.1. While the core essence of Qlik Sense remains same, the new functionalities bring out a more sophisticated and convenient approach to interact and build engaging applications. The new features also boost the self-service functionality of Qlik Sense by providing options such as *Exporting the Stories to PowerPoint* and *Defining variables outside the script using the new Variable interface*.

# Using the visual exploration capability in Qlik Sense® 2.1.1

The visual exploration capability introduced in Qlik Sense 2.1 strengthens the concept of self-service Business Intelligence. It puts more power in the hands of business users or users who are not the original authors of the application. It allows users to change properties of certain objects such as bar charts, scatter charts, and trendline charts without entering the Edit mode or changing the underlying content of the application. The feature works in all versions of Qlik Sense, namely Qlik Sense Desktop, Qlik Sense Enterprise, and Qlik Sense Cloud.

## Getting ready

This recipe will make use of the `Automotive.qvf` application available on the Qlik Sense hub. This application usually comes with the default installation of Qlik Sense Desktop. If you don't get the application with the installation, you can download the same from the source material for this chapter available on the Packt Publishing website.

## How to do it...

1. Open the `Automotive.qvf` application from the hub.
2. Open the `Sales overview` sheet.
3. Hover over the **Vehicle sales by region** bar chart and just beside the fullscreen icon, you will find the **Exploration menu** icon. Click on it.

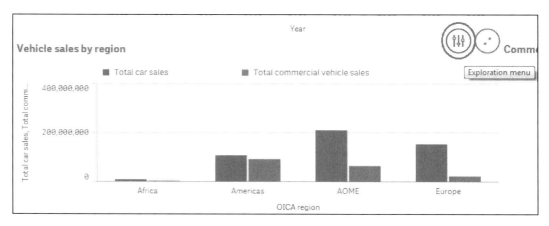

4. On clicking, the object goes fullscreen and while still in the analysis mode, the Properties panel gets activated.

5. In this mode, we can change a subset of properties such as sorting, colors, presentation, and so on.

6. Change the color scheme of the bar chart to Single color.

7. Once done, confirm the changes.

8. Exit the fullscreen mode.

9. The object with the changed properties look like this:

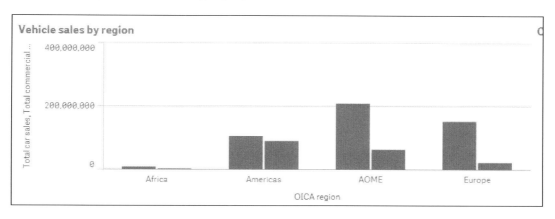

## How it works...

The visual exploration feature allows the business user to change the properties of the onscreen objects without entering the Edit mode. If the user himself is the author of the application, then they can keep the changes and make them a part of the original application.

An end user who is accessing a published application on Qlik Sense Cloud or Qlik Sense Enterprise can make the changes to the properties using visual exploration techniques but can't keep them. In other words, the changes remain only in the users' session.

## There's more...

The visual exploration capability can be used only with certain Qlik Sense objects. It cannot be used with gauge charts, table objects, or pivot charts. It cannot be used with extension objects either.

## See also

▶ *Exporting stories to MS PowerPoint*

# Defining variables in Qlik Sense®

For versions prior to v2.1.1, Qlik Sense does not provide the option to define variables outside the script as you could in the **Variable Overview** window in Qlikview. With v2.1.1, Qlik has introduced a new variable interface that enlists the existing variables created in the script and also provides the user with the option to create new variables.

## Getting ready

For the purpose of this recipe, we will make use of an inline data load which gives the sales information for four countries:

1. Create a new Qlik Sense application and call it `QS_Variables`.

2. Load the following script in the application:

```
Sales:
LOAD * INLINE [
Country, Sales,COS
USA, 1000,500
UK, 2000,1000
France, 3000,2500
Germany, 4000,4700
];

Let vRedColor=RGB (255, 0, 0);
Let vSales= 'Sum(Sales)';
```

## How to do it...

1. Open the `QS_Variables` application.

2. Create a new sheet called as `Sales` and go to the Edit mode for the sheet.

3. While in the Edit mode, notice that we have a new icon on the lower-left corner. Click on the icon to open the **Variables** interface window.

4. The **Variables** interface window lists all the variables that we have defined in the script:

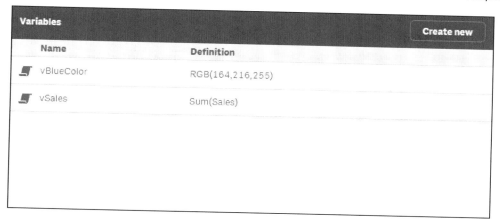

5. At the same time, it gives us the option to create new variables outside the script directly in the interface using the **Create new** button at the top-right corner.

6. Click on the **Create new** button and define a new variable, as shown here:

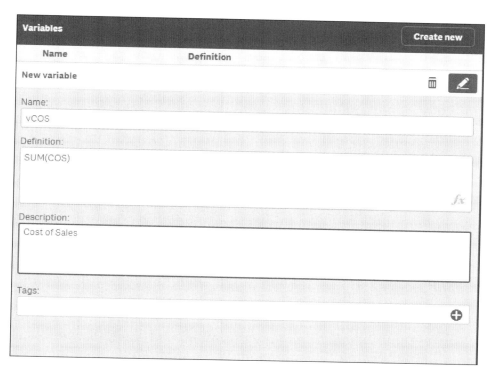

7. Click on the **Save** button and close the variable interface. Reopen to see the list of variables.

8. While still in the Edit mode, drag a table object onto the sheet.

9. Use **Country** as a dimension.

10. Create a measure with the following expression and label it `Sales`:

    ```
    = $(vSales)
    ```

11. Create a second measure with the following expression and label it `Cost of Sales`:

    ```
    =$(vCOS)
    ```

12. Define the background color expression for `Cost of Sales` as follows:

    ```
    =if([Cost of Sales]>Sales,vRedColor,White())
    ```

13. The resulting table would look like this:

| Sales | | | |
|---|---|---|---|
| Country 🔍 | | Sales | Cost of Sales |
| **Totals** | | **10000** | **8700** |
| France | | 3000 | 2500 |
| Germany | | 4000 | 4700 |
| UK | | 2000 | 1000 |
| USA | | 1000 | 500 |

## How it works...

The variables can be put to an effective use in the application to define expressions as well as to store certain field values. If numeric values are stored in the variables, then we don't need to use the $ sign expansion while calling the variables. It is however a good practice to always use the $ sign, as it is needed in case of expression syntax, tests or literals.

A point to be noted in our recipe is regarding the background color expression defined in step no 12. `Cost of Sales` and `Sales` are expression labels we defined earlier and not fields from the Data model.

The background color expression simply references the label of the expressions containing the numbers we need. Referencing an existing expression label instead of repeating the same code can also benefit overall chart performance. This is because Qlik Sense only has to aggregate the values at a base Data model level once; thereafter, the output can be reused from the cached memory where needed.

The variables that are defined in the script are denoted by a  symbol in the variable interface and cannot be edited only through the data load editor, as shown in the following screenshot:

 **vRedColor**

RGB(255,0,0)

This variable is defined in the script. Use the data load editor to edit the variable.

## There's more...

The variables can also be defined in external files such as a text file and then loaded into the application through the data load editor.

In order to try this, complete the following steps:

1. Download the `Variables.xlsx` file from the Packt Publishing website and set up a library connection to the file location called `QlikSenseCookBook_SourceFiles` (to resemble the FROM... code used in the following code).

2. Copy and load the following code:

```
VariableDefinitions:
LOAD
    Variable,
    Expression
FROM [lib:// QlikSenseCookBook_SourceFiles/Variables.xlsx]
(ooxml, embedded labels, table is Variables);

Let vNumberOfRows = NoOfRows('VariableDefinitions');
For vI = 0 to (vNumberOfRows - 1)
Let vVariable_Name = Peek('Variable',vI,'Expression');
Let [$(vVariable_Name)] =
  Peek('Expression',vI,'Expression');
Next
```

If you now go back to the `Variable` list from the edit sheet window, you will see a variable has been created for each row in the Excel file attached. The code below the `FROM` statement simply loops through each row of the Excel file, creating a new variable each time. The values in column *A* become the variable names and the corresponding values in column *B* are used as the variable definitions.

## See also

▶ *Using smart data load profiling*

# Exporting stories to MS PowerPoint

Stories in Qlik Sense are a great feature that can help create insights within data and share those insights with the users in the form of slideshow. These slideshows are native to Qlikview, and hence only users having access to the Qlik Sense application can view the storyline.

With Version 2.1.1, Qlik has introduced the concept of exporting the stories to PowerPoint presentations in order to provide access to users outside the system. Once the storyboard is exported, the users can edit the presentation using the standard formatting functions in MS PowerPoint. One can also print and share the presentation with a larger audience base.

## Getting ready

In *Chapter 2, Visualizations* we created a storyboard using the `Automotive.qvf` application. We will be using the same storyboard to analyze the export function. If you don't have the storyboard saved in the application, you can create one again and then proceed with the *How to do it...* section.

## How to do it...

1.  Open the `Automotive.qvf` application from Qlik Sense hub.

2.  Click on the  button to display the available stories.

3.  Open the Sales Overview story.

4.  From the action menu at the top, select **Export a story to PowerPoint**.

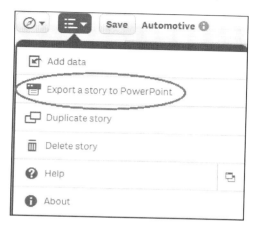

5.  On clicking, the following **PowerPoint Settings** window appears:

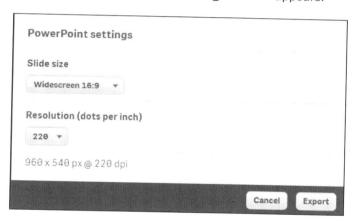

6.  Select the appropriate values for **Slide size** and **Resolution** and click on **Export**.

7. The export process creates a hyperlink that needs to be used for downloading the PowerPoint presentation:

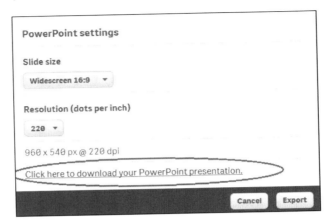

8. Click on the hyperlink to open the storyboard in a PowerPoint file:

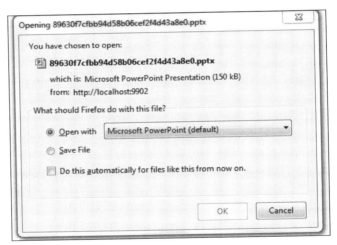

9. Click on **OK** to open the PowerPoint file, which looks like this:

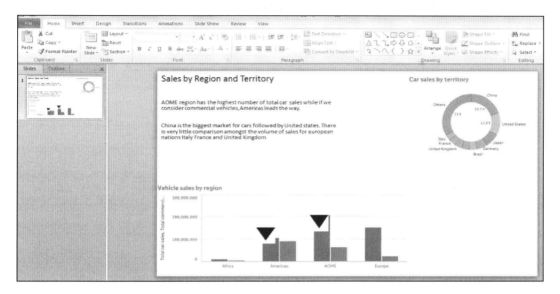

## How it works...

When we click on the hyperlink in the PowerPoint Settings window, Qlik Sense uses the default browser on the system to download and open the story in a PowerPoint file. The export functionality is designed purposefully for the users who don't have access to the Qlik Sense application. As with any other PowerPoint file, you can edit the look and feel of the objects using the formatting functions in PowerPoint.

## There's more...

Currently, the export functionality does not work with the extension objects or the embedded sheets. But this will be possible in future versions of the software.

It has also been noticed that sometimes the wizard takes a long time to generate the hyperlink for the PowerPoint export. In such a case, clear out the cache in your default browser and test again.

## See also

▶ *Defining variables in Qlik Sense®*

# Using the Qlik Dev Hub in Qlik Sense® 2.1.1

Qlik Sense Version 2.1.1 combines the Single configurator, Mashup editor, and the Extension editor under a common single platform called as the **Qlik Dev Hub**. It formally replaces Qlik Sense Workbench used in versions of Qlik Sense prior to 2.1.1 and provides a nice, easy interface to work on these different tools and utilities.

Users who have knowledge of the Workbench editor with prior versions of Qlik Sense must keep in mind that the basic principles of using the Single configurator or creating mashups and extensions remain the same. However, there are subtle changes in the individual interfaces of each of the editors which we will discuss in this recipe.

This recipe will not extensively explain how to create extension objects and mashups or how to deal with Single configurator. However, it will introduce the user to the change in concept when working with Qlik Sense Version 2.1.1.

The next few recipes will be more descriptive in nature and explain the step-by-step process of generating the extensions and mashups using the Qlik Dev Hub. Also, we will discuss the process of embedding Qlik Sense content on a web page using a Single configurator.

## Getting ready

Before starting Qlik Dev Hub, make sure you have Qlik Sense Desktop running in the background.

## How to do it...

1.  Open Qlik Dev Hub using the following URL:

    ```
    http://localhost:4848/dev-hub
    ```

2.  As with the Qlik Sense workbench, we will see that the interface shows all the available mashups and visualization extensions in the form of tiles. Along with this, the left-hand side pane gives access to tools such as **Single configurator**, **Mashup editor**, **Extension editor**, and **Engine API Explorer**:

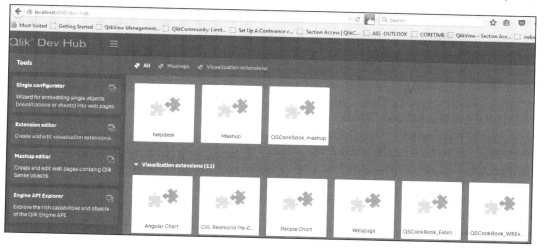

## Single configurator

1. Click on **Single configurator**. The following screen appears:

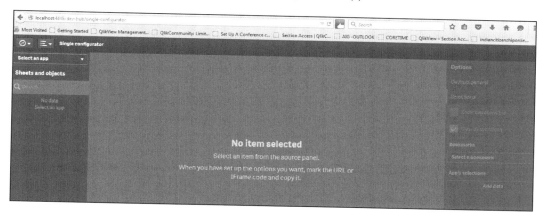

2. The Source panel on the left-hand side lists all the available applications on Qlik Sense hub in the dropdown.

3. Select `MFA interactive.qvf` and then click on the **Car sales by country** chart:

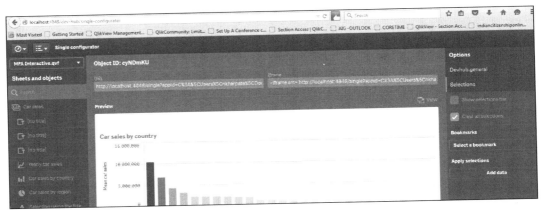

4. As seen, the properties for the chart get activated.

5. The **URL** and **iframe** link are located at the top of the **Preview** window. The single configurator allows the user to access all the Qlik Sense applications and visualization objects and it references them via a URL. The URL can be copied and used in any web browser. The **iframe** link can be used to embed the chart in a website.

6. The **Options** for chart interaction, selections, and bookmarks are in the right-hand side panel. The **URL** and **iframe** links are modified based on the options selected by the user.

## Extensions editor

1. In order to access the **Extension editor**, return to the Dev Hub page by clicking on ⚒ Qlik Dev Hub under the navigation dropdown.

2. Click on **Extension editor** in the left-hand side pane. Contrary to the workbench wherein the extension can be created via the main screen, **Extension editor** opens up a new window:

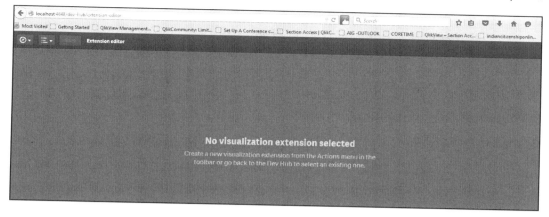

3. In order to create a new extension, click on **Create new project** under the menu on the toolbar:

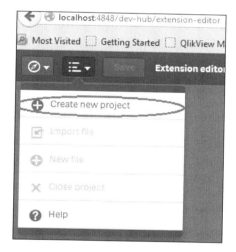

4. On clicking, the following window appears which is exactly similar to the previous workbench version. Here, we can give a name to our new extension and use the basic default templates available with the editor:

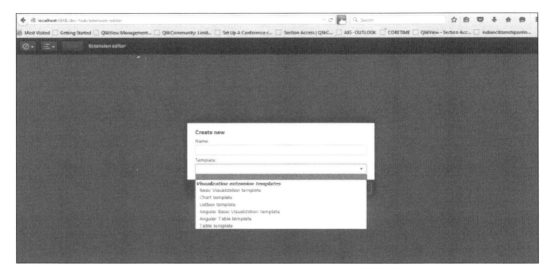

5. Once we define the name and template for our extension object, click on the **Create & edit** button. This opens up the tabs for the JavaScript, `.qext`, and other related files for the extension. If we want to get added functionalities in the extension, we can modify the JavaScript code here as per the requirement.

6. As we develop the extension object in **Extension editor**, the Dev Hub makes it live in the Qlik Sense environment.

## Mashup editor

1. In order to access the **Mashup editor**, return to the Dev Hub page by clicking on **Qlik Dev Hub** under the navigation dropdown.

2. Click on **Mashup editor** in the left pane.

3. The **Mashup editor** interface is very much similar to the **Extension editor** interface.

4. Once we define the name and template for the mashup and click on **Create & edit**, the following window appears:

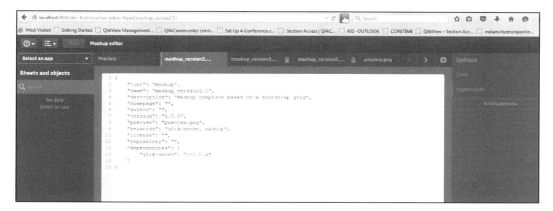

5. We can select the application and visualization objects from the Source panel on the left. The visualization objects can be laid out in the grid by the simple process of drag and drop. There is a menu bar at the top that gives access to the preview window as well as the underlying files for the mashup.

## How it works...

The developer hub is a single platform for creating the extensions and mashups in Qlik Sense. It gives access to JavaScript APIs, which consist of a number of methods and properties to build the custom visualizations. The editors autogenerate the mandatory files required for the extension and mashups to work.

## There's more...

**Qlik Dev Hub** can also be opened by opening **Qlik Sense Desktop** and then clicking on the dropdown option under the menu item at the top:

### Single configurator

While working with the Single configurator, if we use multiple charts in our web page, then all the charts will continue to interact with each other similar to an out of the box Qlik Sense environment.

### Extension editor

For non-programmers, Qlik provides an easy way to amend the extension script files. In order to do that, one can access the example codes at `http://help.qlik.com/sense/2.1/en-us/developer/#../Subsystems/Dev-Hub/Content/Examples/dev-hub-code-examples.htm%3FTocPath%3DQlik%2520Dev%2520Hub|Examples|_____0.`

Select a particular extension under **Examples** and then grab the JavaSript code and the QEXT code for your extension. Make sure you also copy and paste the code for other related files the JavaScript is referring to, for example, the `.CSS` files and the `.PNG` files.

## See also

▸ *Using the Qlik DataMarket*

# Using Extension editor in Qlik Dev Hub

In the previous chapter, we discussed a recipe to develop a visualization extension in Qlik Sense by writing the code manually in the .js and .qext files. One of the easier methods to develop extension visualization in Qlik Sense is using **Extension editor** in Qlik Dev Hub.

A Qlik Dev Hub is an integrated development toolbox used for building visualizations and mashup websites. It does not come with a separate installation package, but the editor and the API libraries are provided with Qlik Sense Desktop.

The previous recipe has explained all the basics of the Dev Hub. This recipe will introduce the user to the process of building a basic chart extension using **Extension editor** in Qlik Dev Hub. The extension workbench supports the .js, .qext, .css, and .html formats.

## Getting ready

For the purpose of this recipe, we will make use of an inline data load which gives the sales information for four countries:

1. Create a new Qlik Sense application and call it QS_DevHub_Extensions.

2. Load the following script in the application:

```
Sales:
LOAD * INLINE [
Country, Sales
USA, 1000
UK, 2000
France, 3000
Germany, 4000
];
```

3. Save the application at this point and move on to build the visualization using **Extension editor**.

4. Before starting **Extension editor**, make sure you have Qlik Sense Desktop running in the background.

## How to do it...

1. Open Qlik Dev Hub using the following URL:

```
http://localhost:4848/dev-hub
```

2. Click on the **Extension editor** / *Create and edit visualization extensions* button available in the left-hand side pane of Qlik Dev Hub.

3. A new **Extension editor** window opens. Click on the menu dropdown ☰▾ on the toolbar.

4. Now, click on ⊕ *Create new project* to create a new project.

5. Name the new visualization as `QlikDevHub_Extension`.

6. Under **Template**, select **Chart template** and click on **Create & edit**:

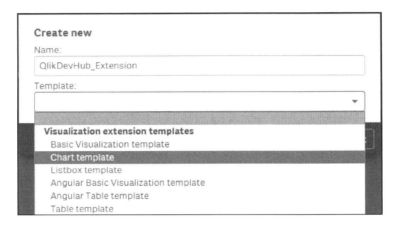

7. This opens up the tabs for the JavaScript, `.qext`, and other related files for the extension. If we want to get added functionalities in the extension, we can modify the JavaScript code here as per requirements.

8. As seen, the editor has automatically created the mandatory files and the script required for the extension.

9. Edit the script on the `QlikDevHub_Extension.qext` tab as follows:

```
"description": "Qlik Sense extension using the Qlik Dev
   Hub",
"author": "<User Name>"
```

10. The result of the preceding code will look like this:

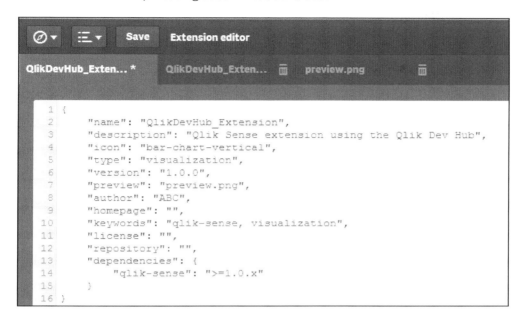

11. The `QlikDevHub_Extension.js` tab contains the JavaScript required for rendering the visualization. One can edit this tab if required to do so.

12. Save and close the window.

13. Open the `QS_DevHub_Extensions` application we created in step 1 of the *Getting ready* section in Qlik Sense Desktop.

14. Create a new sheet and enter the Edit mode by clicking on  ✎ **Edit** .

15. The `QlikDevHub_Extension` extension object is now available in the Assets panel on the left. Drag the extension onto the sheet.

16. Add **Country** as a dimension.

17. Add the following measure:

    `Sum (Sales)`

18. Name the chart as `Sales by Country`.

19. The resultant chart would be as follows:

**Sales by Country**

France: 3000
Germany: 4000
UK: 2000
USA: 1000

## How it works...

The Qlik Sense **Extension editor** provides JavaScript APIs, which consist of a number of methods and properties to build the custom visualizations. The editor autogenerates the mandatory files required for the extension to work.

## There's more...

If we want to define custom styles for our visualization, we can do so by using one or more CSS files. The content for the CSS files first need to be loaded to the document's header or alternatively added as a link to a style sheet to the document's header. Styles can also be defined using the RequireJS CSS plugin.

Additional files such as `.css`, `.js`, and `.html` can be added using the button located at the top-right hand corner of the **Extension editor** workspace:

## See also

▸ *Using Qlik Dev Hub to generate mashups*

# Using Qlik Dev Hub to generate mashups

A mashup is a web page consisting of content from more than one source displayed in a single user interface. When we design mashups in Qlik Sense, we integrate multiple random objects from a Qlik Sense application into a predefined layout. In doing so, we use the active content from the Qlik Sense application. Hence, the visualizations get updated automatically when the state of the object changes.

The **Mashup editor** in Qlik Dev Hub allows us to build mashups using the Mashups API. These Mashup APIs are used to display Qlik Sense objects on a website or web application where one can interact with the Qlik Sense datasets.

## Getting ready

We make use of the `Automotive .qvf` application for this recipe. This application comes with the default installation of Qlik Sense. If not, it is available for download from the Packt Publishing website. Before starting the Qlik Dev Hub editor, make sure you have the Qlik Sense Desktop running in the background.

## How to do it...

1. Open Qlik Dev Hub using the following URL:

   `http://localhost:4848/dev-hub`

2. Click on the 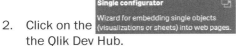 button available in the left-hand side panel of the Qlik Dev Hub.

3. A new **Mashup editor** window opens.

4. Now click on ⊕ Create new project to create a new project.

5. Name the new mashup object `QlikDevHub_Mashup`.

6. Select the template as **Basic mashup template with absolute positioning**:

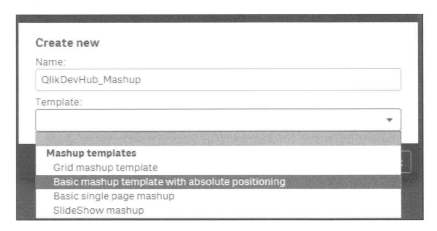

7. Click on **Create & edit**.

8. Once we create the mashup, the **Mashup editor** window reopens. It consists of three panes. The one on the left-hand side gives an option to select a Qlik Sense application on the hub and the objects it may contain. The central pane consists of the **Preview** window for the Mashup Layout and the two main files that help to generate that layout: .html and .js. The Qlik Sense content is stored in the .html file, while the .js script file contains the code for the mashups. The right-hand side pane gives options to add **Lists** and **Hypercubes** to the mashup:

9. In the left-hand side pane, select the `Automotive.qvf` application from the dropdown. Once selected, objects within the application will be displayed.

10. Check 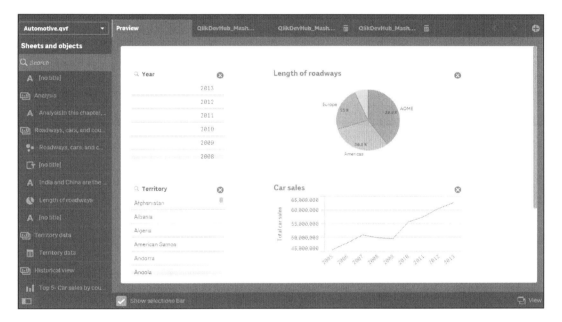 at the bottom of the central pane.

11. Scroll down to the **Roadways, Cars, and Countries** sheet and drag the Filter pane within that sheet onto the layout. This will display the **Year** selection on the layout.

12. Next, drag and drop the **Length of roadways** pie chart onto the layout.

13. Scroll down to the **Country car data** sheet and drag the Filter pane within that sheet onto the layout on the right-hand side. This will display the **Territory** selection on the layout.

14. Drag and drop the **Car sales** trend line chart onto the layout.

15. The layout should look like this:

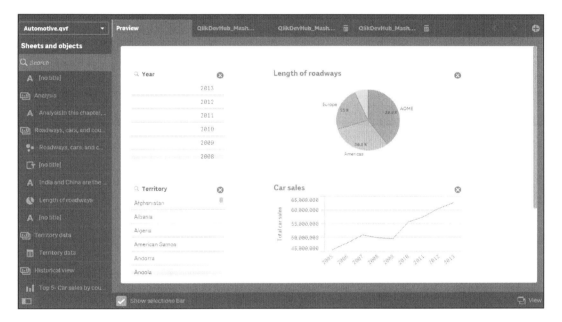

16. In order to preview the mashup, click on the button at the bottom of the central pane.

17. The user can make selections on the mashup page similar to Qlik Sense.

18. Click on **Save**. The mashup page can be launched using the Qlik Dev Hub link, selecting the mashup, and clicking on **View**. Alternatively, the mashup link can be shared amongst the users. For example, in our case, it would be like this:

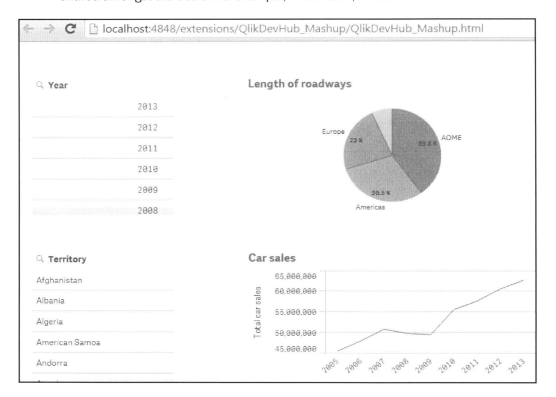

## How it works...

1. When we select the application, in our case, `Automotive.qvf`, the JavaScript in the `QlikDevHub_Mashup.js` file gets updated as the following. Every new application opened will add a new line in the open apps section:

2. When we select the visualizations to display on our mashup page, the `QlikDevHub_Mashup.html` page gets updated. By taking a look at the tab, we can see that the code looks like this:

## There's more...

We can also add lists to the Qlik Sense application using the list builder. The lists are not a part of the Qlik Sense application our mashup is connected to. Along with the lists, we can also add a **Hypercube** with specified dimensions and measures to further enhance our mashups.

Both the options can be found on the right-hand side panel of the **Mashup editor** window.

## See also

▶ *Embedding Qlik Sense® application on a website using a single configurator*

# Embedding Qlik Sense® application on a website using a single configurator

Qlik defines a Single configurator as *a tool that provides an easy way of creating simple mashup pages without having to write any code at all*. It helps to create a URL that contains the embedded Qlik Sense visualization. A user can embed a sheet, an object, or even a snapshot from the Qlik Sense application. The URL can be embedded onto the desired web page using the `iframe` integration or the `Div` integration.

## Getting ready

For this recipe, we will develop a simple HTML page and then embed a Qlik Sense sheet onto the page.

1. In order to generate a web page, copy and paste the following script in a text file:

```
<html>
<title>My Web-page</title>
<body bgcolor="beige">
Qlik Sense
<marquee>Embedding Qlik Sense application in website using
    single configurator!</marquee>
<img src="http://siliconcloud.com/sc-
    content/uploads/2015/06/qliksense.png" height="200"
    width="200"></body>
<html>
```

2. Save the file and name it `QlikDevHub_WebPage.html`.

3. The preceding steps create a simple website that displays a Qlik Sense icon and a rolling marquee displaying **Embedding Qlik Sense application in website using single configurator!**:

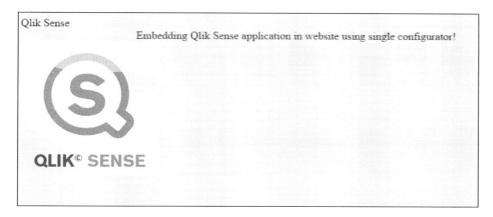

4. Our next step would be to embed Qlik Sense visualization on this sheet.

## How to do it...

1. Open Qlik Dev Hub using the following URL:

   ```
   http://localhost:4848/dev-hub
   ```

   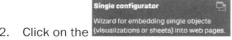

2. Click on the [Single configurator / Wizard for embedding single objects (visualizations or sheets) into web pages.] button available in the left-hand side panel of the Qlik Dev Hub. A new **Single configurator** editor window opens. The source panel on the left lists all the applications available on Qlik Sense hub.

3. From the dropdown, select the `Automotive.qvf` application. Once we select the application, observe that all the sheets and the objects within the application are listed underneath. Any snapshots within the application are also listed under the **Snapshot** tab.

4. Now, select the **Sales overview** sheet from the list. On selecting this sheet, two more panes get activated on the screen. The central pane is a **Preview** window that shows the selected sheet along with the **Preview Object ID** option at the top and a URL that contains the HTML information on the object.

5.  The right-hand side panel gives the user options to activate or deactivate certain properties in the mashup. For example, show the **Selections bar**, **Chart animations**, **Interaction**, **Bookmarks**, and so on:

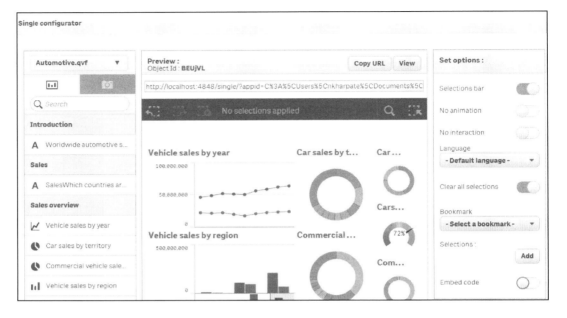

6.  Make the following changes from the right-hand side panel:

    ❏   Under **Devhub.general**, ensure that **Disable interaction** is switched off.

    ❏   Under **Selections**, ensure that the show **Selection bar** and **Clear all selections** are switched on.

7.  The code to be inserted within an `iframe` tag in our HTML script for the web page is autogenerated in the Iframe box just above the **Preview** window.

8.  The code will look something like this:

```
<iframe
  src="http://localhost:4848/single/?
  appid=C%3A%5CUsers%5Cnkharpate%5CDocuments%
  5CQlik%5CSense%5CApps%5CAutomotive.qvf&sheet=
  BEUjVL&opt=currsel&select=clearall"
  frameborder="0"></iframe>
```

9.  Copy and paste it in between the `<marquee>` and `<img>` lines in the HTML script for the web page.

10. We will slightly alter this code for changing the height, width, and the alignment of the frame:

```
<iframe src="http://localhost:4848/single/?
   appid=C%3A%5CUsers%5Cnkharpate%5CDocuments%
   5CQlik%5CSense%5CApps%5CAutomotive.qvf&sheet=
   BEUjVL&opt=currsel&select=clearall"
   frameborder="0"height="600" width="75%"
   align="right"></iframe>
```

11. The final HTML code for the web page should look like this:

```
<html>
<title>My Web-page</title>
<body bgcolor="beige">
Qlik Sense
<marquee>Embedding Qlik Sense application in website using
   single configurator!</marquee>
<iframe
   src="http://localhost:4848/single/?appid=C%
   3A%5CUsers%5Cnkharpate%5CDocuments%5CQlik%5CSense%
   5CApps%5CAutomotive.qvf&sheet=BEUjVL&opt=currsel&
 select=clearall" frameborder="0"height="600" width="75%"
   align="right"></iframe>
<img src="http://siliconcloud.com/sc-
   content/uploads/2015/06/qliksense.png" height="200"
   width="200"></body>
<html>
```

12. Save the changes made in the document.

13. Open the web page to see the embedded Qlik Sense sheet:

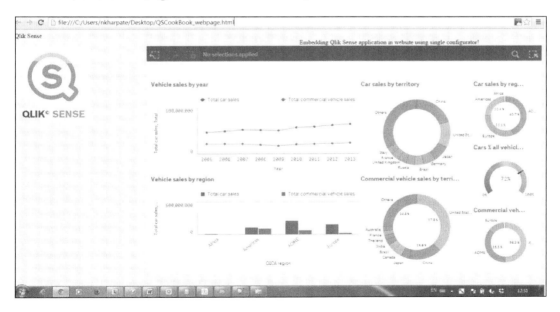

## How it works...

The embedded sheet on the web page works exactly like a sheet within Qlik Sense. The user can make any selection in the charts and the data would be filtered accordingly.

The current selections are displayed at the top. The charts contain active content, and hence they are always in sync with the actual Qlik Sense application.

## There's more...

The `iframe` script inserted in the HTML page can further be modified as required. We can very well add multiple objects from different Qlik Sense applications on the same web page.

Another good option to explore in the configurator is adding data.

We can define explicit field value selections within the `iframe` code. The data on the sheet would always adhere to these selections:

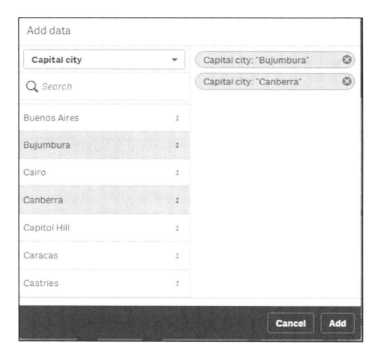

## See also

▶ *Using Qlik Dev Hub to generate mashups*

# Using the Qlik DataMarket

The Qlik DataMarket allows you to source additional data externally. This data is provided by Qlik to enrich your current reporting data set. It is a "data as a service" cloud offering, which allows you to access a collection of different valuable, up-to-date and ready-to-use datasets.

## Getting ready...

For the purpose of this recipe, we will make use of an inline data load which gives the information on sales and the base currency:

1. Create a new Qlik Sense application and call it QS_DataMarket.

2. Load the following data into the QlikSense data load editor:

```
ExampleData:
LOAD * INLINE [
    Base currency, Sales
    US dollar, 6300
];
```

3. Save and reload the application.

## How to do it...

1. Open the QS_ DataMarket application.

2. Create a new sheet called Sales and go to the Edit mode for the sheet.

3. From Qlik Sense Desktop, open the **Data manager** as shown in the following screenshot. Please note that this feature is only available from Version 2.0 onwards.

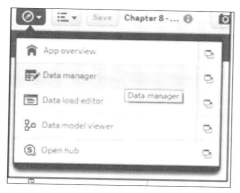

The data manager is a new feature of Qlik Sense. We will cover the different aspects in other recipes; for now, let's look at the Qlik DataMarket.

4. Click on the  button located on the left-hand side of the **Data manager** screen.

5. Next, click on the Qlik DataMarket button.

6. For this example, we will click on the  option.

7. Next, select the 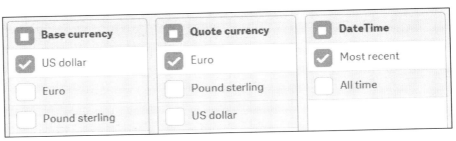 option.

8. The next screen allows you to choose what data you want to load. Select the options as shown in the following screenshot:

| Base currency | Quote currency | DateTime |
|---|---|---|
| ☑ US dollar | ☑ Euro | ☑ Most recent |
| ☐ Euro | ☐ Pound sterling | ☐ All time |
| ☐ Pound sterling | ☐ US dollar | |

9. Click on the **Load and finish** button at the bottom-right corner of the screen.

10. Once the load has finished, go to the application editor and drag a KPI object from the asset pane onto the main content pane.

11. Create a new master item `Measure` with the name `Sales ($)` and the following expression:

```
Sum(Sales)
```

12. Create a second master item `Measure` with the name `Sales` (in selected quote currency) and the following expression:

```
Sum ({<[Quote currency]={$(='[' & GetFieldSelections([Quote
   currency]) & ']')}>}Sales * [Exchange rate])
```

13. Drag the first and second measures onto the KPI object. The final object should look like the following image:

## How it works...

In this example, we enrich the existing internal data set with an external source. Here, we simply add a euro conversion rate from our dollar amounts but we could have added several other currency conversions. The limitations of how much data you can augment to your internal data set is based on the data Qlik provide in the DataMarket, and having the right fields in your internal data set to cross reference to the right DataMarket field. The ones shown in this example are free. To get access to even more data sources in the DataMarket, you have to pay a subscription fee. The price list for these subscriptions can be obtained from Qlik.

The current offerings in the Qlik DataMarket are broken down into six categories:

▸ Business
▸ Currency
▸ Demographics
▸ Society
▸ Weather
▸ Economy

These categories are shown in the following screenshot:

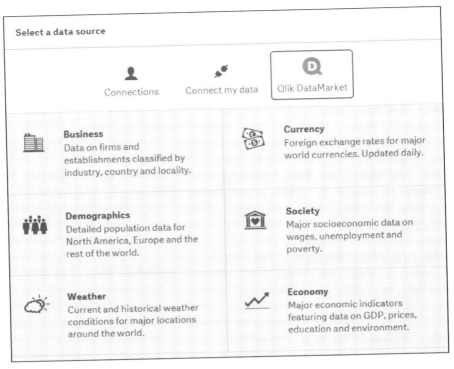

Being able to expand your own core data with that in the Qlik Data Market allows you to take an outside-in view of the business and its environment, helping you to explore and connect market trends to see opportunities and challenges. Qlik plans to keep adding to the DataMarket with more sources in future releases. The data sources are updated in Qlik as they are updated in the source systems. For example, exchange rate information will likely be updated daily, whereas country population data is more likely to be updated annually.

## See also

> *Using the Qlik Dev Hub in Qlik Sense® 2.1.1*

# Creating dynamic charts in Qlik Sense®

To increase the flexibility of a single chart object, you can set it up so that the dimension used is based on what the user wants to see. This is a much more efficient use of space for single sheets and makes the whole experience much more dynamic.

## Getting ready

For the purpose of this recipe, we will make use of the sales information for different fruits as defined in the script:

1. Create a new Qlik Sense application and call it `QS_DynamicCharts`.

2. Load the following data into the data load editor:

```
Transactions:
Load
 Mod(IterNo(),26)+1 AS Period,
 Pick(Ceil(3*Rand()),'Standard','Premium','Discount') AS
  ProductType,
 Pick(Ceil(6*Rand()),'Apple','Orange','Cherry','Plum','Fig',
  'Pear') AS Category,
 Pick(Ceil(3*Rand()),'Heavy','Medium','Light') AS Weight,
 Pick(Ceil(2*Rand()),'2013','2014') AS Year,
 Round(1000*Rand()*Rand()*Rand()) AS Sales
Autogenerate 20
While Rand()<=0.5 or IterNo()=1;

SET vDimension = 'GetFieldSelections(Dimensions)';

Dimensions:
LOAD * INLINE [
    Dimensions
    Weight
    ProductType
    Category
    Period
];
```

## How to do it...

1. From the **App overview**, create a new sheet and enter the Edit mode.

2. Add the field **Dimensions** onto the main content pane.

3. Drag a bar chart object onto the content pane.

4. Add the following expression as a measure:

```
Sum(Sales)
```

5. Add a following calculated dimension by clicking on the $\overline{fx}$ button:

```
= [' &
  Pick(Match($(vDimension),'Weight','ProductType',
  'Category'),Weight,ProductType,Category) & ']'
```

6. Enter one click of the space bar as the label to make it appear as if there is no dimension label.

7. Exit the editor mode and select a value in the **Dimensions** field.

8. The final product should resemble the following screenshot:

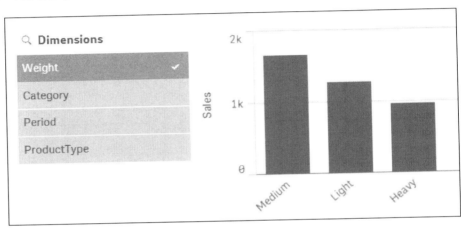

## How it works...

In the script loaded at the beginning of the recipe, we set a variable called vDimension. The GetFieldSelections() function will return the values selected in the field we specify inside the brackets GetFieldSelections (Dimensions). The Dimensions field is simply a hardcoded list of specific fields in the Data model. The code we wrote in the dimension field of the chart uses this variable value to set the dimension dynamically to whatever value the user picks in the list box we created.

## There's More....

If you are running Qlik Sense 2.1.1, then you can now enter expressions in the chart title area. If so, enter the following code:

```
='Showing Sales by: ' & $(vDimension)
```

This displays the selected dimension in the chart title dynamically. If you are running an earlier version of Qlik Sense, simply leave the label blank. After this, I would suggest creating a textbox explaining the chart, which will display whatever the value is, in the associated list box. You can also use the preceding expression in the explanation textbox.

# Using Smart Search

**Smart Search** is a new feature of Qlik Sense. As with most search features, you type in what you are looking for and a list of possibilities are returned. These are based on the field values in your data. This recipe shows you how to tailor what is returned when performing a smart search.

## Getting ready

For the purpose of this recipe, we will make use of an inline data load which gives the release information for different labels. Load the following data in the script load editor:

```
Data:
LOAD * INLINE [
    Label, DJ, Next Album Release, Release Year
    Blunderbuss Records, Kevin Mullaney, The Chat, 2016
    Weirdo Cats, Heather McKay, Unknown,
    Dragon Disks, Rhys Hayward , Unknown,
    Caped Capers, Simon Conyers, No Fashion, 2016
    Shadow Giggles, Ski Mask, Electro Ski, 2015
    Fiddle Pits, Isabel Franken, Boogie Fingers, 2015
];
```

## How to do it...

1. Open the main content pane and click on the [ ] button in the top-right corner.

2. Type `ski` into the search box and note that two values are returned, as shown in the following image:

3. Now, go to the script editor and type in the following code:

   ```
   Search Exclude "Next Album Release", "Release Year";
   ```

4. Save and reload the application.

5. Repeat step 2. This time, only a single value is returned in the smart search results.

## How it works...

In this example, we used the `Search Exclude` function to restrict two fields from the Data model we don't want users to be able to search on. The fields are called `Next Album Release` and `Release Year`. There is also a `Search Include` function, where listing only the fields you want users to search on is simpler than listing those you don't want to include. Examples of fields you would normally exclude are `Key` fields that join the tables in your Data model. Removing unnecessary fields also helps with the performance of searches.

## There's More....

Other than just controlling what fields are accessible via the smart search functionality, there are different ways to perform a search. This involves using special characters other than just typing in the literals you are looking for. Examples are given in the following table:

| Character | Example | Description |
|-----------|---------|-------------|
| " " | "Orange Juice" | Encapsulating the value in quotes makes Qlik Sense search for the whole word instead of *Orange* and *Juice* separately. |
| + | +Orange +Juice | Finds strings that include both words although they can be in any order. Such words could be *Orange and apple juice* or *Juice from oranges*. |
| ~ | ~Orange | This is Fuzzy Search, where the values are ranked and sorted according to the similarity to the search string. This search only works when selecting the search icon for an individual field and does not work in the global search at the top of the screen. |
| >, <, >=, <= | =Sum(Sales)>100 | Expression searches also only act on a single field similar to Fuzzy Search. The results are returned based on the aggregation. Numeric searches such as >01/01/2015 also work without an explicit aggregation function and can be used to narrow down the search. |

| Character | Example | Description |
|-----------|---------|-------------|
| * | Oran* | The * symbol is a wildcard character and will return any values that start with the letters *Oran*. The wildcard character replaces a single or block of characters in a search string. It can be used at the start and middle of a search string, for example, *Oran, Oran*, or *Oran*. |
| ? | Oran?e | The ? character is also a wildcard that represents a single character. |

QlikView also has other types of searches, such as Numeric, Fuzzy, Expression, and Compound Search. I believe these are on the road map, although they are not included in the product to date. To see if these features have been released in later versions of Qlik Sense, please refer to the Qlik Sense online help feature accessed via the hub.

## See also

▶ *Using smart data load profiling*

# Using smart data load profiling

As you know from the earlier chapters on accessing data, Qlik Sense makes associations between tables using similar field names. As of Qlik Sense Version 2.0, there is a data profiling tool that can be used to help you make the correct table associations.

## Getting ready

1. Create a folder on your local drive called `TestData`. For this example, we will use the **C:** drive: `C:\TestData`.

2. Create a folder library connection to the directory above in the data load editor.

3. Load the following script into the application:

```
Transactions:
LOAD DATE(Date#( TransactionDate,'DD/MM/YYYY')) as
    TransactionDate ,Sales INLINE [
    TransactionDate, Sales
    01/01/2013, 1000
    02/01/2013, 3000
    03/01/2013, 500
    04/01/2013, 4000
    05/01/2013, 2000
```

```
];

Calendar:
LOAD DATE(Date#( TransactionDate,'DD/MM/YYYY')) as Date,
    Month,Year INLINE [
    Date, Month, Year
    01/01/2013, Jan, 2013
    02/01/2013, Jan, 2013
    03/01/2013, Jan, 2013
    04/01/2013, Jan, 2013
    05/01/2013, Jan, 2013
];


STORE Transactions INTO
  [lib://TestData/Transactions.txt](txt);
Drop Table Transactions;

STORE Calendar INTO [lib://TestData/Calendar.txt](txt);
Drop Table Calendar;
```

## How to do it...

1. Click the Navigation dropdown button on the top-left and select the **Data manager**, as shown here:

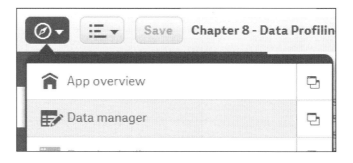

2. Select  from the menu bar on the left-hand side.

3. Click on the **TestData** library connection we established earlier.

4. Select the `Transaction.txt` file as shown here, and click on the next arrow at the bottom of the page:

↩

▤ Transactions.txt

5. You will see a preview of the data to be loaded. Click on **Load and finish** at the bottom of the page.

6. Once loaded, you will return to the data manager and the transactions table will be listed on the left. Let's load the second table. Repeat steps 2, 3, and 4 only. Click on the `Calendar.txt` data this time.

7. Instead of clicking on the **Load and finish** button, click on the ⟨ Profile > ⟩ button.

8. Click on the  option.

9. Under the Rename fields option, click on the button labeled **TransactionDate**.

10. Click on **Load and finish** in the bottom-right hand corner.

11. Close the execution window and click on **Save**.

12. If you open the Data model viewer from the main hub menu now, the two tables should now be joined, as shown here:

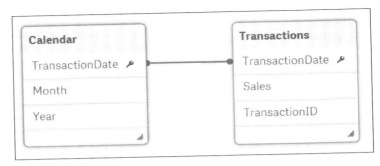

## How it works...

The script we loaded at the beginning of the recipe simply generates the data we use in the data load editor. The profiler looks at these data files to make recommendations on fields you should use to join the two datasets together. In this example, there is only one suggestion made, which is for the **TransactionDate** field and the **Date** field.

If there are more, you can step through the various suggestions using the arrows in the load editor page. This is shown in the following screenshot:

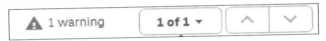

Our example identified that there is a 100 percent match on the values contained between both of our data sets but the name of those fields are different. As such, one or both of the fields need to be renamed in order to associate the tables. The fields were renamed automatically when we clicked on the button labeled **TransactionDate**. We could have entered a new name for both fields by typing in the **Rename both fields to** box.

There are several other warnings the data profiler will make you aware of, depending on the data you load. One example is if there were fields with the same name but data that didn't match. Another example is if there are multiple possible connections you could make; in this example, the profiler will recommend you to either keep one of the fields as a key then rename the others, or break the table association.

## There's More....

The Data manager allows you to bring in data and make associations from a number of sources without ever seeing a line of code. The code is still present, but it is generated automatically and saved in a system generated script tab. After completing this recipe, open the data editor to see the new tab, as show in the following image:

It is also worth making clear that the data profiler works without finding 100 percent matches on shared field values between tables. To test this, repeat the recipe with the following line of code added to the end of the transactions table in the *Getting ready* section of the recipe:

```
6, 06/01/2013, 100
```

The profiler works in exactly the same way as recommending the correct field link, but now it will inform you there is a **91%** match between the values contained in both tables:

# Conclusion

With this we come to the end of this book. This book is a small effort to help tackle day-to-day issues faced by Qlik Sense developers. We have introduced the users to some of the key traits of Qlik Sense through recipes. The book travels through the basics of Qlik Sense to more advanced scripting, calculations, and extensions. Keeping in mind the importance of User Interface we have also dealt with a few recipes related to the best practices in design of a Qlik Sense application.

We don't undermine the fact that there may be many different ways to overcome the challenges discussed in some of the recipes but we have tried to present the best approach in this book.

The knowledge shared in this book is something that we have experienced and learnt over the course of many years of business intelligence implementations. We believe that learning never ends and having worked with Qlik product suite for so long, we are still learning new things every day. In fact, even while writing this book, both of us exchanged many ideas, which in a way were helpful in expanding our knowledge base.

Having said that, our learning is more valuable only when it is shared with others. This book is the source of sharing our thoughts with the wider world.

We would consider our efforts to be worthy if the aspiring as well as experienced Qlik Sense developers find our book helpful.

Wish you an enjoyable journey with Qlik Sense..!!

# Appendix

The following keyboard shortcuts assume the use of MS Windows. For Mac OS, use *Cmd* instead of *Ctrl*:

| Shortcut | Action |
| --- | --- |
| *Ctrl + P* | This prints the current view or active sheet/story. |
| *Ctrl + C* | This copies the selected item to the clipboard. |
| *Ctrl + X* | This cuts the selected item and copies it to the clipboard. When using the Google Chrome browser, if the cursor is put in front of a row in the data load editor or in the expression editor, without selecting anything, the entire row is cut. |
| *Ctrl +V* | This pastes the most recently copied item from the clipboard. |
| *Ctrl +Z* | Using this combination, you can undo an action. You can repeat it to undo earlier actions. |
| *Ctrl +Y (Cmd + shift + Z* for Mac OS) | Using this combination, you can redo actions. |
| *Ctrl + H* | This opens the online help in the context of the current function, while in the data load editor or the expression editor. |
| *Ctrl + F* | This opens smart search. |
| *Ctrl + E* | In the sheet view, this opens and closes the editing of the selected sheet. |
| *Ctrl + S* | This saves changes to the app. |
| *Ctrl + O* | This opens an app copied to the clipboard using *Ctrl + C.* |
| *Ctrl + A* | This selects all the code in the data load editor. |

| Shortcut | Action |
|---|---|
| Ctrl + D | This deletes the content of the current line in the data load editor or in the expression editor. |
| Ctrl +K | This comments or uncomments the selected lines in the data load editor. |
| Ctrl + OO | This inserts a test script in the data load editor. |
| Tab | This indents the code in the data load editor. |
| Shift + Tab | This outdents the code in the data load editor. |
| Left arrow | This navigates to the previous slide in the storytelling view. |
| Right arrow | This navigates to the next slide in the storytelling view. |
| Up arrow | This scrolls up in a table. |
| Down arrow | This scrolls down in a table. |
| Ctrl + left arrow | This navigates to the previous sheet in the sheet view. |
| Ctrl + right arrow | This navigates to the next sheet in the sheet view. |
| Ctrl + up arrow | This navigates to the first sheet of the app in the sheet view. |
| Ctrl + down arrow | This navigates to the last sheet of the app in the sheet view. |
| Esc | This exits play mode in the storytelling view. This deselects a visualization when editing in the sheet view. This deselects an object. This undoes selections in a visualization. This closes a dialog or window. |
| Delete | This deletes the selected item. |
| Backspace | This deletes the selected item. |
| Enter/Return | This performs the actions for the active option or button (for example, in dialogs). |
| Ctrl + + | Using this combination, you can zoom in. |
| Ctrl + - | Using this combination, you can zoom out. |
| Ctrl + 0 | This resets zooming. |

# Index

**Data model viewer**
associations, viewing  18, 19
Data model, viewing  18
data, previewing  17
master library, creating from  20-27
table meta data  19
**data points**
navigating, in scatter chart  115-117
**Declare function**
used, for generating Calendar fields  142-144
**Derive function**
used, for generating Calendar fields  142-144
**dimensionless bar charts**
creating, in Qlik Sense®  102-104
**distribution  54**
**dynamic charts**
creating, in Qlik Sense®  244-246

## E

**E() function**
using, in Set Analysis  181-184
**embedded functions**
using, in Set Analysis  173-175
**embedded sheets**
adding, to story  39, 40
**Expression editor**
help, invoking  15, 16
**extended interval match**
used, for handling Slowly Changing
Dimensions  120-126
**Extension editor**
using, in Qlik Dev Hub  227-230
**extensions**
data, using with  200-206

## F

**field values list**
capturing, concat() used  180, 181
**files**
extracting from folders,
For Each loop used  148-150
**files, Qlik Sense® extension**
.JS file  188
.QEXT file  188

**FirstSortedValue() function**
used, for identifying median in
quartile range  140, 141
**flags**
using, in Set Analysis expressions  163-165
**For Each loop**
for loading data, from multiple files  76-78
used, for extracting files
from folders  148-150
**Fractile() function**
used, for generating quartiles  138-140

## G

**geo maps**
creating, in Qlik Sense®  88-93

## H

**HTML visualization extension**
creating, for Qlik Sense®  188-193
**HyperCube  205**

## I

**Image**
creating  107

## K

**keyboard shortcuts, Qlik Sense®
desktop  255, 256**
**Keyhole Markup Language (KML)  88**
**Key Performance Indicators (KPIs)  41**
**KPI object**
using, in Qlik Sense®  96-99

## L

**latest record, for dimensional value**
identifying, Previous() function used  126, 127
**limitations**
applying, to charts  110-113
**line-level table  132**

## Thank you for buying
## Qlik Sense® Cookbook

# About Packt Publishing

Packt, pronounced 'packed', published its first book, *Mastering phpMyAdmin for Effective MySQL Management*, in April 2004, and subsequently continued to specialize in publishing highly focused books on specific technologies and solutions.

Our books and publications share the experiences of your fellow IT professionals in adapting and customizing today's systems, applications, and frameworks. Our solution-based books give you the knowledge and power to customize the software and technologies you're using to get the job done. Packt books are more specific and less general than the IT books you have seen in the past. Our unique business model allows us to bring you more focused information, giving you more of what you need to know, and less of what you don't.

Packt is a modern yet unique publishing company that focuses on producing quality, cutting-edge books for communities of developers, administrators, and newbies alike. For more information, please visit our website at www.PacktPub.com.

# About Packt Enterprise

In 2010, Packt launched two new brands, Packt Enterprise and Packt Open Source, in order to continue its focus on specialization. This book is part of the Packt Enterprise brand, home to books published on enterprise software – software created by major vendors, including (but not limited to) IBM, Microsoft, and Oracle, often for use in other corporations. Its titles will offer information relevant to a range of users of this software, including administrators, developers, architects, and end users.

# Writing for Packt

We welcome all inquiries from people who are interested in authoring. Book proposals should be sent to author@packtpub.com. If your book idea is still at an early stage and you would like to discuss it first before writing a formal book proposal, then please contact us; one of our commissioning editors will get in touch with you.

We're not just looking for published authors; if you have strong technical skills but no writing experience, our experienced editors can help you develop a writing career, or simply get some additional reward for your expertise.

# Learning Qlik Sense

## The Official Guide

ISBN: 978-1-78217-335-9        Paperback: 230 pages

Get to grips with the vision of Qlik Sense for next generation business intelligence and data discovery

1. Get insider insight on Qlik Sense and its new approach to business intelligence.

2. Create your own Qlik Sense applications, and administer server architecture.

3. Explore practical demonstrations for utilizing Qlik Sense to discover data for sales, human resources, and more.

# Mastering QlikView

ISBN: 978-1-78217-329-8        Paperback: 422 pages

Unleash the power of QlikView and Qlik Sense to make optimum use of data for Business Intelligence

1. Let QlikView help you use Business Intelligence and data more effectively .

2. Learn how to use this leading BI solution to visualize, share and communicate insights.

3. Discover advanced expressions and scripting techniques that will help you get more from QlikView.

## Predictive Analytics Using Rattle and Qlik Sense

ISBN: 978-1-78439-580-3          Paperback: 452 pages

Create comprehensive solutions for predictive analysis using Rattle and share them with Qlik Sense

1. Create visualizations, dashboards, and data applications with Qlik Sense and Rattle.

2. Load, explore, and manipulate data to Rattle to create predictions and discover hidden patterns in the data.

3. A step-by-step guide to learning predictive analytics in a quick and easy way.

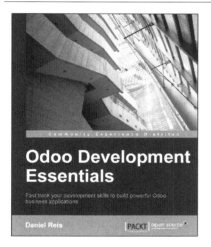

## Odoo Development Essentials

ISBN: 978-1-78439-279-6          Paperback: 214 pages

Fast track your development skills to build powerful Odoo business applications

1. Leverage the powerful and rapid development Odoo framework to build the perfect app for your business needs.

2. Learn to use models, views, and business logic to assemble solid business applications effectively.

3. Get up and running with Odoo and integrate it with external data and applications using this easy-to-follow guide.

Please check **www.PacktPub.com** for information on our titles

11143804R00155

Printed in Great Britain
by Amazon